17680

WITHDRAWN

F
MIL
c.3
$15.00

WITHDRAWN

Me and My Name

Me and My Name

BY MARY JANE MILLER

toExcel

San Jose New York Lincoln Shanghai

Me and My Name

Published by toExcel
an imprint of iUniverse.com, Inc.

For information address:
iUniverse.com, Inc.
620 North 48th Street
Suite 201
Lincoln, NE 68504-3467
www.iuniverse.com

ISBN: 0-595-00330-3

Printed in the United States of America

For my family with love and gratitude.

One

Last night, on what I thought was an ordinary Thursday, Leo, my stepfather, came home and said, "It's all set. I talked to the lawyers today and the adoption papers will be coming tomorrow."

Mom's eyes went all misty.

"Great," I said, trying to gulp down a lump as big as a basketball.

We went to Dino's, our favorite restaurant, for a celebration dinner. "To our daughter," Mom and Leo said. They gave me a mushy look as they clinked their glasses.

They clinked their glasses again. "And to the baby." Mom is expecting in September.

Mom and Leo went on clinking and toasting every-body, even Lincoln, our dog. I concentrated on eating my spaghetti. I wasn't sure I'd ever get it down, but I knew if I didn't eat it, Mom and Leo would know some-thing was wrong.

And they'd be right.

When we came home, Mom and Leo wanted to talk about the adoption, but I told them I had to study for Mrs. Lewis's fifty-word monster spelling test.

Instead of studying for the test, I sat on the floor of my closet and wrote my name in red marker on the back wall. Under my name I wrote a message. *Erin Mitchell wrote her name on this wall when she was almost twelve years old.* It probably sounds like a weird thing to do, but I wanted my name to be someplace where I could go and see it.

If Leo adopts me, I won't be Erin Mitchell. I'll be Erin Zanin. And when you've been Erin Mitchell all your life, how can you turn into Erin Zanin?

What a mess, I thought. Why did Daddy tell Mom and Leo it was okay with him if Leo wanted to adopt me? Just thinking about it made my stomach hurt.

When Mom and Leo came into my room to say good night, I didn't say much. Mom looked at me and asked, "What's wrong?"

2

I don't think it's fair that mothers can look at your face and know that something is going on in your head. I shrugged and said, "Spelling. I'll probably get zero-minus F on my test tomorrow." It wasn't a lie. I'm the world's worst speller. And it was easier to talk about spelling. I couldn't get the word *adoption* out. It was stuck behind my teeth.

Leo laughed. "You worry too much, punkin. If there was a worldwide worry-wart contest, I'd put my money on you."

Mom gave me three kisses, one on each cheek and one on the nose. She said, "No more fussing. Get some sleep."

After they left, I closed my eyes. They popped right open. I closed them again. My eyes kept opening and closing. I started watching the clock. When it blinked 12:12, I yelled for Mom. Mom and Leo came running into my room.

"What's wrong?" Leo asked in a sleepy voice.

"I can't sleep." I felt dumb, silly, and sick. I shouldn't have shoved down all that spaghetti. I told them I might barf and I wasn't sure I wanted to be adopted.

Mom and Leo gave each other one of those looks. It was the same kind of look Lincoln gives me when I say, "No more cookies." Why did I open my mouth? Who said "honesty is the best policy"?

After about a century, Mom and Leo said they understood. I didn't really believe them because Mom kept biting her lip and Leo started pulling on his mustache. They both said to think about it for a little while longer and then decide.

I wished I knew what to do. I wanted Mom and Leo to be happy, but I didn't know if I could ever get used to being Erin Zanin.

Leo kissed me good night. Mom sat on my bed and ran her fingers through my hair. I wanted to crawl into her lap and tell her how mixed-up I felt but an eleven, almost twelve-year-old kid sitting on her mother's lap would look pretty weird, so I didn't do or say anything.

After a while, Mom said, "I love you, Erin. Leo loves you, too. Everything will work out."

How, I wanted to ask, but I didn't.

I guess Mom wanted to change the subject, so she asked me if I had thought of any more names for the baby. Mom has this thing about names. We took out every name book in the library last week. We've been thinking about Susan if it's a girl and John if it's a boy.

I shook my head. I've been having enough trouble with my own name, I thought, pulling the covers up to my neck.

"Names are important," Mom said, as if she were talking to herself. Maybe that's why Mom and Leo want me to be adopted. Maybe Mom thinks we can't be a family if the baby and I have different last names.

As soon as Mom left the room, my stomach started to

hurt again. I wanted to yell, "Mom, come back," but Mom doesn't need two babies. So I dragged Fluffy, my teddy bear, out from under the bed, hugged him tight, and closed my eyes.

My eyes wouldn't stay closed. I started watching the clock again. 12:33. 12:38. I wondered if Jenny, my best friend, was awake. It would be fun if we each had our own telephones and could call in the middle of the night. I didn't want to talk to Jenny tonight, though. She'd ask me if I had decided. She thinks it's wonderful that I can change my name.

"It's just like getting married," she said. "You'll even impress Kim Adams."

"Oh, sure," I said. "The same day it rains jelly beans." Kim Adams is only the most popular girl in the sixth grade.

The clock blinked 12:59. I turned on the radio and then turned it off. Mom and Leo would know I was still awake if they heard the radio blaring. I turned over and punched my pillow three times. That didn't help so I got up, wandered over to my dresser, and stared at Daddy's picture. He stared back.

I picked up my lucky penny and flipped it. Last fall, Leo and I found my penny when we were raking leaves. I flipped my penny three more times, put it down, opened my pajama drawer, and pulled out Daddy's letter.

Even though I must have read it at least two hundred

times, I read it again.

Hi, Erin,

Good news. I'm going to be in Florida for a while. I hope you can come down for a visit. I'd like to show you where the sea turtles lay their eggs, and there's a dolphin I want you to meet.

I suppose you've been wondering what I think about Leo's plan to adopt you. You sounded a little worried when we talked. The adoption plan is okay with me if it's okay with you. It won't change the fact that you'll always be my little girl.

Love,
Daddy

How can Daddy still think I'm his little girl? Little girls aren't 5 feet, 6 inches tall. And besides, Daddy doesn't really know me. He hasn't seen me in six years.

If I went to visit him, he'd probably walk right past me in the airport and I'd have to say, "Excuse me, I'm your daughter."

I crawled back into bed, punched my pillow again, closed my eyes, and started counting sheep.

Sheep are very boring, so I started counting chocolate-covered candy bars with peanuts. After I counted 103 chocolate bars, I switched to Rocky Raspberry Double Bubble chewing gum. Then I fell asleep.

Two

When Mrs. Lewis handed back my spelling test, she didn't say anything, she just yelled at me with her eyebrows. Mrs. Lewis has straight black eyebrows that go up and down when something bugs her.

I jammed my test into my spelling folder. *F*'s are very depressing.

"Jenny," I whispered. Jenny sits two rows over and one seat ahead of me. She didn't hear me. She was too busy looking at her test. I was sure Mrs. Lewis put a gold star on Jenny's test instead of a big red *F*. Jenny always gets *A*'s.

I tried again. "Jenny." She still didn't look up, so I wrote her a note.

Hi, Jenny,
    I can't wait for you after school. I have to practice for my piano lesson.

Your friend,
Erin

P.S. Mrs. Lewis has lipstick on her teeth.

While Mrs. Lewis put the homework assignment on the board, I passed my note by way of Richard Fraizer. He didn't look at my note. Richard is nice that way.

Everyone likes Richard, especially me. I've never told anyone, not even Jenny, that I like Richard. Richard likes Kim Adams and Kim Adams likes Richard. They'll probably get married.

Richard and Kim are the perfect couple. Richard is tall, has curly, dark brown hair, and blue eyes. Kim is short, pretty, and blonde. All she has to do is smile at any boy in Eastmore Junior High and he melts. Even the eighth-grade boys, who usually don't admit that sixth-grade people exist, go out of their way to talk to Kim.

I wish I could get to know Kim. Maybe some of her magic would rub off on me. It's a pretty big maybe, though, because I'm tall and bony and boys like short, curvy girls. Mom says the angles will turn into curves.

I doubt it. I expect to go through life looking like a geometry lesson.

My foot kept tapping until the bell rang. I was the first one out. Richard must have passed my note because I didn't see Jenny.

On my way home, I started playing, "Who should I be? Who should I be?" with the cracks in the sidewalk. Mitchell or Zanin? Mitchell or Zanin?

"Hey, Erin. Wait up."

I turned around. Jenny was running after me. She was huffing and puffing. Jenny's a little overweight.

Last Thursday, in gym class, I heard Kim Adams and Andrea, Kim's best friend, call Jenny Thunder Thighs. Jenny heard it, too, but she just laughed it off. I thought it must have hurt, at least a little bit.

"I've been chasing you for two blocks," Jenny croaked out. "Why didn't you wait?"

"I couldn't. Didn't you get my note?"

"What note?"

"Oh, no," I groaned. I could see Richard handing the note to Mrs. Lewis, saying, "I found this." I felt sick.

But Richard wouldn't do that. He probably forgot to give it to Jenny. But what if it fell out of his pocket? Mrs. Lewis could find it.

"Don't worry," said Jenny. "I'll write a note saying, *Dear Erin, Mrs. Lewis's perfume smells like rotten bananas.* Then we'll both have to go to Hansen's office."

"Thanks, Jenny," I said. "You're a real friend."

"I know," said Jenny, grinning. "So how come you didn't wait for me?"

"I have to practice for my piano lesson. I didn't practice yesterday."

I've been stuck playing Minuet in G Minor for two months. Catherine, my piano teacher, said my head and my fingers weren't getting together.

"You could have waited," Jenny said. "I've been dying to know."

"About what?"

Jenny stared at me. "You know. You promised to tell me. Did you decide to get adopted?"

"No," I answered. I ran across the street wishing Jenny wouldn't bug me. I must have the world's biggest mouth. Why did I tell Jenny I didn't know if I wanted to change my name?

"Won't your stepdad be mad if you don't let him adopt you?" Jenny asked, hurrying to catch up with me.

"No, he won't be mad," I snapped. "He said it was up to me."

"Well, you don't have to go and get all huffy," Jenny said. "What's the matter with you, anyway? You're acting like a real rag."

"Nothing's the matter," I answered crossly. Part of me wanted to tell Jenny that I was going nutso trying to figure out what to do about me and my name. Another

10

part of me didn't want to say anything. That part won. Some things you can't share even with your best friend.

"What's going on with Amy?" I asked Jenny, to change the subject. "Does she have a new boyfriend?" Jenny's sister has a new boyfriend just about every other week.

"Yeah," answered Jenny, rolling her eyes. "He's punk. And," she giggled, "he wears a gold hoop earring. My dad almost turned purple when he came over last night."

We talked about Amy until we reached our corner. Jenny turned right and I turned left. "Call me tonight," Jenny yelled after me as I started running toward home.

When I opened the front door, I knew Mom wasn't there. The house had that funny kind of quiet that shouts, "Nobody's home." There was a note on the kitchen cabinet.

It said:

Hi, Erin,

I've gone to the doctor. If I'm not home by 5 o'clock, please put the casserole in the oven, make a salad, and set the table.

Say "Hi" to Catherine for me. Hope you had a good day. See you soon.

Love ya,
Mom

11

I peeked into the refrigerator. Eggplant Parmigiana. Ugh. Leo likes the strangest food. Maybe I could talk Mom into letting me have a hot dog.

Munching on an oatmeal and raisin cookie, I wandered into the living room, wishing I didn't have to practice the piano. I almost choked on my cookie when I saw the large envelope with the return address of SMITH & CRAMER, ATTORNEYS-AT-LAW, sitting with the rest of the mail on the coffee table.

The adoption papers. I picked up the yellow envelope as if it were a firecracker ready to pop. I didn't know I was going to hide it in my pajama drawer. It just happened. Then I sat on my bed and kept staring at my dresser drawer, expecting the envelope to jump out.

Go practice the piano, dummy, I yelled at myself. After playing two measures of Minuet in G Minor, I gave up and went back to my bedroom.

Very slowly, I opened my pajama drawer. The envelope was still there. I banged the drawer shut and almost knocked Daddy's picture off my dresser. "I don't know what to do," I said to his picture when I picked it up.

Daddy smiled at me from his picture. I stared at him, wishing I could really see him.

"Do you really want me to get adopted?" I asked his picture. I didn't get an answer.

Three

My piano lesson was awful. Catherine didn't say anything, but Tinker, Catherine's cat, hid behind the drapes and didn't come out until I stopped playing. I picked her up and sat down next to Catherine on the sofa.

I wanted to tell Catherine about the yellow envelope from the lawyers, but I didn't know how to begin. Finally, I blurted out, "I can't decide."

"What can't you decide, pet?" Catherine asked in a soft voice.

"If I should be adopted. I don't know what to do."

Catherine patted my hand and said, "It's a tough decision."

Just telling her made me feel a little better. Some kids might think it's weird to have a friend as old as Catherine but I don't care. And anyway, Mom says sixty-five isn't old. And Catherine says friendship doesn't have anything to do with age.

"Let's talk about it over some tea," Catherine said.

After the kettle boiled, Catherine handed me a cup of chamomile tea. I took a little sip. It wasn't too bad. It tasted better than it sounded.

"When do you have to decide?" she asked.

"I don't know," I answered, shaking my head. "Soon." I shrugged my shoulders. "Maybe tomorrow."

Catherine lifted her teacup. I could tell she was thinking because she gets a funny little line between her eyebrows. Mom calls it a frown furrow.

I stared into my teacup and watched a tea leaf float around. Catherine always makes tea with leaves. She never uses tea bags. I guess that's because her grandmother taught her to read the tea leaves when she was a little girl. It's something like reading palms or telling fortunes.

"Could we read the tea leaves?" I asked.

Mom says tea-leaf reading is okay if you do it just for fun. But I think Mom believed the tea leaves when Catherine saw a heart in Mom's teacup. Catherine told Mom

14

that the tea heart meant Mom and Leo would love each other forever.

I hope Catherine's right. I'd miss Leo if he went away. He yells a lot, but he's big on hugs, baseball, and telling Mom and me he loves us.

Mom met Leo right after the divorce four years ago. They met in the hospital emergency room where Mom's a nurse. Mom said anyone as klutzy as Leo is shouldn't go barefoot in the kitchen. Leo almost cooked his foot when he spilled a pan of spaghetti on it.

When Mom and Leo were married, he promised Mom that she could do all the cooking. Leo and I clean up the kitchen and trade school stories. He teaches history to high-school seniors. I don't think I'd mind taking history if Leo were my teacher. He makes it fun. He knows all kinds of stories about kings, queens, presidents, and pirates.

I finished my tea in two gulps and showed my cup to Catherine. She looked into my cup, smiled, and said in a deep, mysterious voice, "I see a letter."

I peered into the cup and pretended to see a letter, too, but all I saw was a glop of tea leaves.

But if Catherine was right, maybe I would get a letter, a letter from Daddy. It would say, "No daughter of mine can change her name." Then I wouldn't have to decide what to do.

"How do you decide to do something?" I asked Catherine.

She folded her hands and put the tips of her fingers against her mouth before she answered. Catherine's not a quick-answer person.

"Sometimes I make a list," she said. "I put the pros, that's why I should do something, at the top of the paper and the cons at the bottom. Then I draw a line between them. I write down my reasons, pro and con, add them up, and the answer is right in front of me."

"I'm going to try it," I said.

"Good," Catherine said, giving my shoulder a little pat. "Now how about another try at Minuet in G Minor?"

When I got home, Mom was back. I gave her a quick kiss and a hug. Every week there's more and more of her to hug.

"What did the doctor say?" I asked.

Mom didn't answer. Her face looked funny, as if she was trying to figure out a puzzle. My stomach started sending me signals. Maybe there was something wrong. Mom's old to be having a baby. She's thirty-five. I knew because I saw her age in the family Bible.

"It's twins, Erin," Mom said in a whisper.

Twins. I gulped. Two Zanins.

"That's great, Mom." My voice squeaked.

Two babies when I was still trying to get used to the idea of one.

"Just wait until your father hears," Mom said in a faraway voice.

16

"Daddy?" I asked.

Mom gave me a spacy look. I reached down and retied the laces on my gym shoes. I felt stupid, really stupid. Mom meant Leo. She never talks about Daddy.

I could feel my cheeks burning. I didn't want Mom to see my face turning red. She'd ask me a ton of questions, so I muttered, "I've got lots of homework," and started out the door.

Mom didn't say, "It's Friday and you never do homework on Friday." She didn't say anything. Maybe she didn't hear me say *Daddy*. I think the news about the twins sent her into the twilight zone.

In my room, I crashed into my bed and hugged Fluffy, my teddy bear. "We might have to move," I whispered into Fluffy's ear, "down the hall to the little room. The twins will need this room. It's bigger."

I wondered if there was really room for me, especially if I stayed a Mitchell.

Four

Pros and cons. Mitchell or Zanin. I chewed my pencil and thought of all the reasons I should be a Zanin.

1. It would make Mom and Leo happy.
2. The twins won't wonder who I am. They might if I have a different last name.
3. No one will stare at me, frown, and say, "I thought your name was Zanin."
4. Maybe Richard Fraizer will notice me if I have a new name.

5. Maybe Kim Adams will invite me to one of her famous sleepovers. She's never invited me as Erin Mitchell.

Next, I wrote the reasons I shouldn't change my name.

1. It would make Daddy sad.

I put down my pencil and picked up Daddy's picture. He must care, just a little, if I change my name. He said I'd always be his little girl. Daddy smiled at me from his picture. I put it down and went on with my list.

2. I'm used to Mitchell.
3. I'd be embarrassed if someone called, "Hey, Zanin," and I didn't know they meant me.
4. Z's are always last. I hate being last.
5. If my name is Zanin maybe I won't feel like me.

I sucked on the eraser part of my pencil. Does a new name make you a new you? What will happen to the part of me that used to be Erin Mitchell if I become Erin Zanin?

I looked at the list. It wasn't going to work. Five pros and five cons stared up at me.

You're a real airhead, Erin Mitchell. How could I think a piece of paper would give me the right answer? Catherine is smart, that's why it worked for her. It felt good to tear up the list into tiny little pieces and throw them into the wastepaper basket. I watched them float to the bottom, wishing they would disappear like soap bubbles going down the kitchen drain.

My stomach grumbled and growled. I could smell bacon and French toast. Mom always cooks bacon on Saturdays.

When I went into the kitchen, Mom said, "The mail came and there's a letter for you."

"There is?" The tea leaves were right. It must be from Daddy. But he never sends small blue envelopes.

It was an invitation. An invitation from Kim Adams to one of her famous sleepovers. It thought I was going to die. It must be a mistake. But it was addressed to me. *Erin Mitchell, 444 Summerdale, Lilac Grove, Illinois, 60148.*

I picked up the phone to call Jenny.

"Erin," Mom said, "your breakfast will get cold. Who are you calling?"

"Jenny."

"Call her after breakfast." Mom looked at the invitation. "Who is Kim Adams?"

"She's the most popular girl in sixth grade. She's the prettiest and the richest, too. Jenny says she probably wears designer underwear."

Mom raised her eyebrows. "Do you like her? You've never asked her over."

I picked at my bacon. "I like her. Can I go to the party? Please."

"Who's going?"

"Everyone. I guess."

Mom looked at the invitation again. She frowned, then smiled. "I remember Kim's mother. She's the jewelry designer who spoke at the P.T.A. luncheon."

"Mo-om. Can I go to the party? Please."

"Yes, if you really want to go," Mom said.

I really didn't know if I wanted to go. I just knew I had to go. An invitation from Kim Adams was the same as an invitation to the White House. You can't say no. My hand started to sweat when I picked up the phone to call Kim.

"Hi, Kim," I said, hoping my voice didn't squeak. "This is Erin Mitchell. Thanks for the invitation. I can come."

"All right," answered Kim. "I'm glad you're coming."

"Who's going to be there?"

"Everybody. Bring two candles, matches, a box of tissues, your sleeping bag, a picture of someone special, and a flashlight. See you in school and see you Friday night."

I grabbed a cookie from the cookie jar and ate it in one gulp. Why did Kim invite me? She's the most perfect of the perfect group. Kim always knows what to do and say. Her tongue never trips over her teeth.

Lincoln came out from under the kitchen table and stared at the cookie jar. "Do you think she's decided to like me?" I asked Lincoln. He kept staring at the cookie jar.

I gave him a chocolate-chip cookie, his favorite kind, and thought about Kim some more. It was weird getting an invitation from her. She's probably said three words to me this year. "Move over," when we were in line in gym class and "Hi," last week in lunch line. I felt creepy when she nudged Andrea, her best friend, and Andrea started laughing and then kept staring at me all through lunch.

I wondered if Jenny got an invitation. What if she didn't? I wasn't sure I wanted to go to Kim's by myself. Lincoln barked for another cookie. We shared the last one before I called Jenny.

It took her a long time to come to the telephone. Her voice crackled when she answered. "I've got a sore throat. My mother is drowning me in orange juice and salt-water gargle. What's up?"

"Did you get any mail this morning?" I asked her, crossing my fingers.

"From who?"

"Kim Adams."

"Are you serious? Why would I get a letter from her?

We never even talk to each other, so she'd never write me a letter. Did she write you?"

"She invited me to a sleepover Friday."

"You're kidding," Jenny squeaked. "Who else is going? Did she invite Laurie or Susie?"

"I don't know."

"Didn't she tell you?"

"No, she just told me what to bring: candles, matches, and a picture of someone special. Do you think I should go?" I hated the idea of going to Kim's without Jenny, but I didn't know what else to do. I had already told Kim I'd go.

Jenny didn't answer me right away. I could hear her blowing her nose. Then she said, "I don't know. It's probably going to be one of those parties."

"What do you mean?"

"You know. Smoking and a séance. My sister Amy heard about a party where they put someone in a trance. . . ." Jenny started coughing.

"Jenny!" I yelled. "Tell me what happened."

"They had to call the paramedics."

"Did she come out of the trance?"

"I don't know. Amy didn't tell me. I have to go. My mom is yelling. She says talking on the phone will hurt my throat. Call me."

I leaned against the wall, thinking about trances. What if you never came out of one? You could grow old just sitting there. You'd have to blink your eyes to let people know you were alive.

I was practicing blinking my eyes when Leo came into the kitchen. "Do you have something in your eye?" he asked.

"No," I answered, feeling silly. I ran the faucet for a drink of water.

"How about a trip to Lincoln Park Zoo this afternoon?" Leo asked. "And then we could walk along the lake."

"I can't," I said. I hoped he wouldn't be too disappointed. Leo loves zoos, even the monkey houses which really stink. And he loves Lake Michigan. He says it reminds him of the ocean. "I have to go to the library. Mrs. Lewis gave us a poetry assignment. *Yuck!*"

Leo laughed and said, "It could be worse."

"How?" I asked. "She's making us memorize a poem, say it out loud, and give a report on the life of the poet."

At the library, I looked up *séance* in the dictionary, after I asked the librarian how to spell it. "Séance: A meeting at which people try to get messages from the dead." I don't know anyone who is dead, except Great-Uncle Brian, and I met him only once before he died.

I walked over to the card catalogue and found the poetry drawer. There must be a million poets. While I was thumbing through the cards, trying to find one that wasn't too boring, I got the funny feeling someone was watching me.

I turned around and saw Ryan Williams standing just inside the door. He smiled and walked toward me.

"Hey, Mitchell," he said, "find a poet yet?"

"No," I answered. "They all look boring." I glanced at the book in his hand. "Do you have yours?"

"Not for the report." He showed me the title of the book he was holding. *Sherlock Holmes Through Time and Space*. Ryan is a real Sherlock Holmes fan. He even belongs to a Sherlock Holmes fan club.

Once, when Mrs. Lewis was checking addresses, Ryan said, "You have mine wrong. It's 221 B, Baker Street."

Mrs. Lewis gave him her eyebrow look and said, "I know where Sherlock Holmes lives. Where do *you* live?" Then she sent Ryan down to the principal's office. "Insolence is not allowed in my classroom," she said, glaring at us. She wrote "insolence" on the board. We had to look it up in the dictionary and use it in a sentence. I wrote, "Insolence means a smart mouth and a smart mouth can get you in trouble."

"I'll help you find a poem," Ryan said.

I looked up at him. Ryan is tall, taller than me, and has red hair and freckles, lots of them. We go to the same Sunday-school class. We're the only two kids from Eastmore Junior High in the class.

We found a book by someone named Emily Dickinson. Her poems looked short. Ryan held up the book and said in a perfect imitation of Mrs. Lewis, "Poetry, boys and girls, enriches the mind." Ryan even raised his eyebrows like she does.

That broke us up. Mrs. Crane, the librarian, heard us and said, "*Shhhh.*" I could feel my cheeks growing hot.

Ryan laughed and said, "Let's go."

The beeper went off as we started through the door because I forgot to check out Emily Dickinson. I left the book on the counter and ran.

"I'm hungry, are you?" asked Ryan as we rode past Dairy Delight.

"Not really," I answered, even though my stomach was rumbling. I had only two dimes and three pennies in my pocket.

We stopped and Ryan went up to the window. He came back with two caramel turtles.

"Can't eat two," he said grinning. "Have one."

It really tasted good. I licked the back of my spoon to get every drop of chocolate.

"See ya," Ryan said when we got to the park.

I thought about Ryan all the way home. I didn't think about Kim Adams or Richard.

Five

What a week. On Monday, I passed my spelling test. I was surprised Mrs. Lewis didn't faint. On Wednesday, Ryan walked me to my locker three times and today, Friday, Richard said "Hi" in the hall twice. Then, at lunch, Kim and Andrea said, "See you tonight."

I peered into the mirror. Why couldn't I look as good as Kim Adams? She didn't have light brown eyebrows and almost nonexistent eyelashes.

I crawled under my bed and pulled out *Beautiful You*. Jenny thought it was a total waste of three dollars but I told her *I need all the help I can get. Beautiful You* doesn't have much help for people who can't wear makeup, though.

Mom said, "Makeup is not an issue open to discussion this year. See me next year."

But I can't wait until next year. If I show up at Kim Adams's party with a naked face, she'll think I'm a complete dork.

I looked at the clock blinking away the minutes. One hour to get ready. I decided Mom is so busy thinking about the twins she'll never notice a little eye shadow and mascara.

Kim always wears mascara. I heard her tell Andrea that she likes Midnight Blue best. Mom wears basic brown. I took her mascara out of the bathroom and peered into the mirror again. When I twirled the wand against my eyelashes, it went into my eye instead.

I ran into the bathroom and splashed my eye with cold water, then hot. What if I'm blind, Mom will kill me.

When my eye finally opened, it was red. Tomato red. Tears were running out of it. It hurt as much as the time I dripped hair conditioner into it. I held a washcloth over my eye and dialled Jenny's number. "I have a red eye. I can't go to the party with a red eye. What should I do?"

"How did you get a red eye?"

"With mascara."

"Red mascara?"

"No," I answered, patting my eye. "When I put on my mom's mascara, I stuck it into my eye. If my mom finds out, I'm in trouble."

"Put a tea bag on it."

"Huh?" I asked. Jenny must have flipped out.

"I saw it on TV," said Jenny. "Mister Michael, the one who does all the make-overs, said tea bags help red eyes."

"Thanks, Jenny. I'll call you tomorrow."

My eye was still stinging when I sat down on the floor, tilted my head back, and put two tea bags on my eyes.

I tried to think about Richard, but all I could think of was how hard it is to swallow when your head is tilting toward the ceiling. Lincoln came in and licked the back of my neck. I jumped up and the tea bags fell off.

I called Jenny back. "It's not working."

"What's not working?"

Sometimes Jenny lives in another world. "The tea bags."

"Did you wet them?"

"No, you didn't tell me to wet them. My eye looks disgusting. Kim is going to laugh at me. What am I going to do?"

"Wet the tea bags and don't worry. You'll get zits if you worry and besides, Kim Adams is too stuck on herself to notice your red eye."

I looked in the mirror again. No big red zits, just one red eye. I wet the tea bags, carried them back to my bedroom in a towel, and flopped down on my bed. The tea bags felt good on my eye.

When Mom knocked on my door, I stuck the tea bags under my pillow. "It's almost seven-thirty," she said. "Need any help?"

"I'm almost ready." I jumped off the bed. That was a close call. I was afraid to look in the mirror, but I did. Jenny was right, a wet tea bag works. My red eye was pink. Maybe there's hope.

I pulled my green nightshirt with my name on it out of the drawer. It looked old and ugly, so I put it back.

The yellow envelope peeked out from under my old blue pajamas. My stomach started flip-flopping just looking at it, so I spread my green nightshirt on top of it. No one has mentioned the adoption since Mom found out about the twins.

I grabbed my shirt with the frog that says, *OH, WART A BEAUTIFUL MORNING* and stuffed it into my backpack.

Was I forgetting anything? I looked at the list of things to take to Kim's. I checked off sleeping bag, pillow, toothbrush. I forgot my toothbrush.

I'd croak if Kim Adams said I had dragon's breath. I wrapped my toothbrush in tissue and put it in my backpack. Next, I checked off flashlight and matches. I thought about taking the fireplace matches, they're easier to light, but Kim and her friends would laugh at me if I brought them.

Everything on the list was packed except a picture of someone special. Who's special? Richard is special. But I don't have a picture of him. And besides, I'd rather die than let Kim and her friends know I like him.

I took Daddy's picture off my desk and stuffed it into my backpack.

"Are you ready?" Leo yelled up the stairs. He gets antsy if he thinks you're going to be late. I guess that's because he's a teacher and has to be ready when the bell rings.

"Almost," I yelled to him. Now that it was time to go, I really felt scared. What if no one talked to me?

What if they made me smoke? Jenny and I tried her father's cigarettes once. Just to see what it was like. We were afraid to light them, so we just stuck them in our mouths and puffed. They tasted like the wads of cotton the dentist stuffs in your mouth.

I wished I was going to spend the night at Jenny's. She invited Susie McKenna and Laurie Conto over to watch *Star Wars* again.

Why did I tell Kim I'd go to her party? It's funny how mixed-up things can get. Last week, I would have died for a chance to go to one of Kim's sleepovers and now that I'm going, I'm not sure I want to go. I wonder why she invited me.

Six

When Leo pulled into the driveway, he leaned across the seat and kissed me. "Have fun, punkin. Call me when you want to be picked up."

I gave him a hug and headed for Kim's house.

Everyone who belonged to the popular group—Sara, Lisa, Andrea, Patti, and Stacey—was standing in the hall under the crystal chandelier, when Kim opened the door.

"I'll take your things," said Kim. "We're going to be in the family room." The family room was bigger than my house. There was an entertainment center, a bar that ran across a wall, and blue carpeting so deep I felt like I was sinking in it up to my teeth.

I sat down next to Sara. She's pretty nice by herself. She cheered and hugged me when I made the winning basket for our team in gym. Our lockers are across from each other, so we've talked. And once, we traded lunches. She hates Swiss cheese and I hate peanut butter with grape jelly, so it worked out. I don't know what she's like at a party, though.

A tall, skinny woman with her hair in a bun came into the room. "Are you girls hungry?" she asked.

"Yes!" we shouted.

"Good," she said, and left the room.

"Is that your mother?" I asked Kim.

Kim turned red. Everybody laughed.

"Let me show you a picture of my mother," Kim said. She took me down a long hall to the library. I knew it was the library because the walls were covered with books. Over the fireplace there was a picture of a woman with long blonde hair.

"That's my mother," Kim said.

"Oh," I said. "She's beautiful." I felt like Dork of the Year.

"Ann is the housekeeper. Don't you have a house-keeper?"

I wondered if floors ever open up so you could fall through and disappear. I could feel my face getting hot.

Kim walked out the door and I followed her to the family room. Ann, the housekeeper, was setting out the food. Nachos, pizza, popcorn, and soda pop.

Everyone grabbed a piece of pizza. It was the kind I hate, pepperoni and mushroom. I bit into a corner and it burned the top of my mouth. I could tell this was going to be the longest night of my life.

When we finished eating, Kim put the Gruesome Crew on the stereo. We started dancing. Sara smiled at me and so did Stacey. Maybe it wouldn't be as bad as I thought.

We were right in the middle of really moving when Kim stopped the stereo. "Okay, guys," she shouted. "It's time!"

"Time for what?" I asked.

Kim pointed to the shuttered door at the end of the room. "Go into the bathroom until we call you," she said.

The bathroom was as big as my bedroom. I sat on a white stool and waited. A blue china frog with a bar of soap in its mouth stared at me. I could hear everybody whispering and laughing.

Kim called, "Come out. We're ready."

I opened the door slowly. The room was dark. I could hear everybody breathing. Beams of light hit the ceiling. Everyone was in a circle waiting for me.

"Step into the circle," Kim said in a spooky voice. "Stick out your finger."

Everyone turned their flashlights on my pinky finger. My hand started shaking. All of me started shaking.

"Swear you will never open your mouth and tell your parents about tonight. What we do is our business."

I gulped and nodded and hoped it wasn't something that would get me in big trouble.

"Say it out loud," Kim said.

I swore, then Kim handed me a needle and a piece of paper. "This is a blood oath. Sign your name and mark it with your blood."

I poked my finger.

"Poke again, harder," Kim said. "Don't be such a baby."

My finger started to bleed. Blood, my blood, was dripping on the paper. I signed my name, marked it in blood and prayed I wouldn't faint.

When I was six, I had to go to the hospital for a blood test. After they stuck me with a giant needle, the nurse asked Mom a question. While they were talking, I fell off the chair. The hospital had a fit. I had to have my head X-rayed. I guess they thought we were going to sue them.

I should have had my head X-rayed for coming to this party.

"This is gross," I said. Everybody laughed and Sara handed me a tissue.

"What are we going to do first?" Patti asked.

"You'll see," said Kim. She went over to the desk. We

all watched her. She opened a drawer and took out a package of cigarettes.

How do I get out of this, I thought, as she handed everyone a cigarette. I'll barf for sure if I have to smoke.

"Get your matches, Erin, and light my cigarette," Kim said in an obey-or-die voice.

I struck the first match. It flared up. Thank you, God. I put it to Kim's cigarette. Nothing happened. The match went out. "Light it again," she said.

This was a living nightmare. Everyone was watching me. How could they know I was afraid of matches? My hand started to shake as I struck another match and put it to Kim's cigarette. Kim puffed and sucked in her cheeks. I kept waving the match around the cigarette until it started to burn my fingers.

"You dummy!" Kim yelled as I dropped the match on the carpet. "My dad will kill me if there's a hole in the carpeting. He paid fifteen thousand dollars for it."

"What's going on here?" Ann, the housekeeper, stood in the doorway. Her face was one big frown.

"Nothing," said Kim. She stretched out on the floor. "We were just playing a game."

When Ann left, everybody but me started smoking. I leaned against the sofa wondering what was going to happen next. Maybe they'll try a séance. Calling up a ghost would be more fun than smoking.

Andrea started fooling around with my backpack.

36

"Let's see what Erin packed," she said. She unzipped my backpack and Daddy's picture fell out.

Kim picked it up. "Who's this?" she asked, holding up Daddy's picture. "I know, it's Erin's someone special. Who is he, Erin? A new rock star?"

Everybody started laughing. I wanted to punch her out. "He's my dad," I said. I tried to grab Daddy's picture from Kim, but she passed it on to Andrea.

"Be serious." Kim laughed. "The guy in the picture is gorgeous. I saw your father. He's almost bald and definitely not a hunk."

Yanking Daddy's picture out of Andrea's hand, I said, "He's my real father." I hated explaining, but I didn't know what else to do. "Leo is my stepfather."

Why did I bring Daddy's picture to this party? It had to be the dumbest thing I'd ever done. No, coming to this party was the dumbest.

"You'll have to introduce us," said Kim. She sounded impressed. "Your father looks like Bruce Springsteen with a beard. Does he play the guitar?"

I didn't answer her. I don't know if he plays the guitar or anything else. How could I tell them I really didn't know my father?

"Where does he live?" asked Stacey. She poked me with her elbow. "We'll go and visit him."

"He lives in Florida, sometimes. He's a photographer, so he travels a lot."

Having them ask questions about Daddy was as bad as having the dentist poke around your mouth.

"Let's call him up," said Kim.

"It's too late." The grandfather clock in the corner showed it was ten-thirty. "It's an hour later in Florida. He might be sleeping."

"We can try," said Kim, her eyes flashing. "This is going to be a blast. Give me his number."

"Come on, Erin, give Kim the number. Don't you want to talk to your father?" Everybody crowded around me.

I gave Kim Daddy's number.

Seven

Kim dialled the number, then handed me the telephone. It rang ten times. "No one is home," I said and hung up.

Kim dialled again. This time Daddy answered.

"Hi, Daddy, it's Erin."

"Where are you? Are you all right?" Daddy asked in a sleepy voice.

"I'm fine," I said. "I'm at Kim Adams's sleepover. She said I could call you. I just wanted to say hi." I couldn't tell him my stomach hurt and I wanted to go home.

"I'm glad you called," said Daddy. "I've been thinking about you."

"Hi, Mr. Mitchell." Everyone crowded around the phone. "Come and visit Erin soon."

" 'Bye, Daddy," I said. I could hear him still talking as I hung up the phone. My hand was shaking. I wondered what Mom and Leo would think if they knew I called Daddy.

"This party is getting B-O-R-I-N-G," said Kim. Everybody turned to look at her. I wondered how you get to be cool like Kim. You must be born that way. "It's time for Truth or Dare," Kim said, pretending to be a radio announcer.

Truth or dare, that's like asking someone if they want to be a meal for a gorilla or a shark. Some choice.

We sat on the floor. Kim closed her eyes and made a circle in the air.

Please, God, don't let her pick me.

Kim pointed to Patti, not me. Whew!

Patti covered her face with her hands and peeked through her fingers. She started to giggle. "Dare," she said and groaned.

Kim got up and went to the bar. She came back with two cans of beer. "Chugalug," she said to Patti.

Patti's eyes grew as big as beach balls. She shook her head. "I can't."

"Are you afraid Mommy and Daddy will find out and scold their little girl?" Kim said.

"Patti's a chicken, Patti's a chicken," everyone started chanting.

Patti flipped off the top and put the can to her mouth. She started to drink. The beer ran down her chin.

"Chugalug, chugalug," everybody yelled but me. I was watching Patti's neck muscles go in and out. I'd drown if they dared me to chugalug or I'd barf all over everybody and everything.

Patti threw down the can, jumped up, and ran into the bathroom. We could hear her barfing.

Kim rolled around the floor laughing. "Hurry up, Patti," she yelled. When Patti came out, she looked green.

Kim started going around the circle again. I closed my eyes. *Don't let it be me. Please don't let it be me.*

"Truth or Dare," Kim shouted. I opened my eyes. She was pointing at me. I was dead meat.

I couldn't choose dare, I'd barf for sure. And choosing truth was scary. "Decide!" they screamed. I started to say truth, but nothing came out of my mouth.

"Since you can't decide, I will, " said Kim. She looked at everyone in the circle. I got a funny feeling they all shared a secret.

"Truth," Kim commanded. Everybody laughed. Why did I come to this dumb party?

Lisa stood over me. She folded her arms across her chest and asked in a solemn voice, "Who do you like?"

Andrea laughed. Kim frowned at her and said, "Shut up."

I gulped and bit my tongue. They know. I know they know I like Richard Fraizer. And he belongs to Kim.

"If you don't tell the truth, your tongue will turn black," said Stacey in a spooky whisper.

"Truth. Truth," they all started to chant. "You like Richard. Admit you like Richard."

I didn't say anything, but I could feel my cheeks turning red. Now I knew why Kim invited me to her party. She wanted to find out if I liked Richard. Why does she care? Richard likes her, not me. Everybody knows that.

"How much do you like him?" Kim asked.

I shook my head. I wanted to die. My whole body felt like it was burning up. "I don't like him. I don't!" I shouted. I could feel tears starting. I blinked them back. What if they spread it around school that I like Richard? He'll never talk to me again.

"I don't like anybody," I said, digging my fingernails into the palm of my hand, hoping God wouldn't count this as a lie.

"Do you dream about Richard kissing you?" Kim asked. "He's kissed me." She flipped back her hair and smiled at me.

I hated her. I could feel the tears starting to spill out

42

of my eyes. I had to get out of there. As I jumped up and ran for the bathroom, I heard Andrea whisper to Stacey, "Wait till Kim tells Richard Stick Mitchell is in love with him. He'll die."

I wanted to die when I closed the bathroom door. The bathroom smelled of puked-up beer. It made me gag, but I couldn't go back. I turned on the fan and splashed cold water on my eyes and wrists. Then I looked in the mirror. My neck was one big red splotch.

"Hurry up, Erin. I have to go," Stacey yelled, pounding on the door. I didn't have a choice. I had to go back. *Please, God, let them forget about Richard and me.*

I opened the door for Stacey. No one looked at me when I came out. They were still playing Truth or Dare. Sara was it. Everybody was watching her. She looked scared. She picked truth.

Andrea screamed when Sara confessed she kissed Jacob La Monti, the class creep, in third grade.

"Girls, quiet down." Ann the housekeeper stood in the doorway, wearing a green-and-yellow-striped robe. Her face looked fierce. I don't think she likes Kim or us. "It's eleven-thirty," she said. "Get ready for bed."

Kim stuck out her tongue at Ann as she walked out. "What a rag," she said. "I'll be glad when my parents get back from Italy. They've been gone for two months. Ann thinks she's my boss. My mother will set her straight."

Kim picked up her hairbrush and ran it through her hair. Lisa yawned and stretched out. "What are we going to do now?" she asked.

"We have one more Truth or Dare planned," said Kim, pointing her finger at me. "You're it, Erin. I get to pick what you do."

Everybody started giggling. I felt sick.

"Dare," Kim said in a loud voice. "Everybody has to do a dare the first time they're invited to one of my parties."

I gulped as she handed me the phone. What if she wanted me to call Richard. It was almost midnight. "Call up your fat friend, Thunder Thighs, and ask her if lightning strikes when her thighs bump together."

I could feel everyone's eyes watching me, wondering if I'd do it. "Jenny's in bed," I answered, feeling stupid.

"You have to call her. It's a dare." Kim handed me the telephone. My hands started to sweat. I didn't know what to do. Then I got an idea. Maybe it would work. I dialled Kim's number. "It's busy," I said, holding up the receiver so they could hear.

"Try again," said Kim. "I'll help you. What's her number?"

Lisa pulled out a piece of paper from her backpack. They planned to do this. How could they be so mean? How could I have been so stupid to think Kim wanted me to come to her party because she liked me? Kim

44

dialled the number and handed me the telephone. I could hardly hold it, my hand was so sweaty. It started to ring.

"Hello," Jenny's father answered. He sounded mad.

I hung up.

Everybody was watching Kim to see what she would do.

"Call back," she said in a sticky-sweet voice. "And if you don't, you're going to have to call someone to come and get you. No one breaks a dare at my house."

I didn't know what to do. I bit my lip so hard it tasted salty. Everyone was watching me except Sara. She was staring at her fingernails.

I picked up the telephone and started dialling. Leo answered.

"Could you come and get me?" I asked. "I don't feel very well."

Eight

The next morning at breakfast, I opened my big mouth and told Mom and Leo I had called Daddy from Kim's.

"You called your father from Kim's," Mom said in an I-don't-believe-you're-telling-me-this voice. She put her coffee mug down on the kitchen table with a loud clank.

Leo's ears turned red and he yelled, "Why did you do that?"

"I don't know. I just did," I yelled back. I hate fights and I could tell this was going to be a big one.

I tried not to cry. I bit my lip hard and dug my nails into my hand. It didn't work. The tears kept coming. Everything: Kim, Richard, Daddy, the yellow envelope, started churning around inside. I tried to stop crying, but I couldn't.

Mom and Leo jumped up and came over to me. Mom hugged me and Leo patted my hand and said, "I'm sorry I yelled. It's okay, punkin. Everything is okay."

I shook my head. "No. It's not. I stole your envelope."

"What envelope?" Leo frowned.

"The big yellow one from the lawyers."

"You took it?" Leo asked sharply. I gulped and nodded. I could tell by the look on Leo's face that he was one second away from yelling again.

"Why did you do that?" Mom asked. Her voice sounded puzzled and her face looked sad.

"I don't know. I just did." I sniffled. I knew what I said sounded stupid but I didn't know what else to say. It was the truth.

"Erin," Leo said, "we started this adoption business so you'd know I think of you as my daughter. I do. You do know that, don't you?"

I nodded yes.

"Good. Now . . ." Leo stopped for just a minute and then said, "We'll put the adoption on hold for a little while."

Leo looked over at Mom. I could tell they were talking

with their eyes. Mom nodded. She came over to me and wiped my face with a warm washcloth. "Don't worry about the adoption. Whatever you decide is all right with us. We love you."

I snuggled in close to Mom. She smiled at me and brushed my hair out of my eyes. "Where your father is concerned, I get a little crazy," she said. "I have to remember, he's part of you."

I was glad the fight was over. Fights always give me a stomachache. I sort of remember Mom and Daddy fighting. Why did they have to get so weird? Being their kid is like trying to roller skate through a tornado.

Leo brought me a glass of water. "Feeling better?" he asked.

Just as I started to say yes, a giant pain in my stomach turned the yes into an "Ohhh." It was the worst stomachache of my whole life. It hurt more than the time Jenny and I pigged out on a large cheese-and-sausage pizza and two dishes of Rocky Road ice cream. Mom and Leo thought it might be appendicitis. I kept holding my right side. That's where it hurt the most.

All the way to the emergency room, Mom kept her arm around me. "Old-fashioned bellyache," the doctor said. I wasn't lucky enough to have appendicitis. If I did, maybe Kim Adams wouldn't hate me. Maybe everyone would come to the hospital to see me. Even Daddy.

Tuesday morning, Mom said, "Sorry, no choice. You have to go to school today."

I told Mom my stomach still hurt. "You'll be fine," she said with a smile.

How could she be so sure?

When Leo came into the kitchen for a glass of orange juice, he said, "Things have a way of working out."

"Can you work it out so I don't have to see Kim Adams ever again?"

"Honey," Mom said, "we're proud of you. You could never hurt Jenny's feelings. You did the right thing." Mom gave the oatmeal she was cooking a quick stir and turned to me. "It must have been hard to do."

"Don't let Kim and her friends scare you," Leo said. "Compared to you, they're not even worth a monkey's flea. Remember that." I laughed a little. Leo gets carried away sometimes.

Mom spooned oatmeal into a dish for me and said, "School might not be as bad as you think. Things seldom are."

"Oh, sure," I said putting brown sugar and milk on my oatmeal. "And I'll win the next spelling bee."

I know Mom and Leo are trying to help me, but it's hopeless. Kim is going to tell everyone I'm a chicken. Or, they'll hold an election and vote me in as Dork of the Year. And worst of all, I know they're going to tell Richard Fraizer I like him.

A magic button would come in handy now. I'd zap myself down to Florida and Daddy. Then I wouldn't have to go to school.

No magic button popped up, so I had to leave for school. Jenny was waiting for me at the corner. She was wearing her red sweater. Wearing red to school on Tuesday is the same as wearing a "yes" button. Everybody knows that.

"Jenny," I started to say, "what will . . . ?"

"No one is going to tell me what to wear on Tuesday or any other day," Jenny said, giving me one of her come-off-it looks. Jenny really has it all together. She knows exactly who she is. I wish I did.

"Why couldn't you tell me about the party on the telephone?" Jenny asked.

I could tell by the way she asked, she was mad at me. I looked down at my gym shoes and watched my shoelaces bounce as we walked. I didn't say anything.

"Tell me," Jenny said impatiently.

"I can't. I took a blood oath."

Jenny looked hurt. "I'm your best friend," she said. "You can tell me."

"I can't. A blood oath is more than a promise."

Jenny and I walked half a block without saying anything.

"I've got it!" Jenny yelled. "I can take a blood oath not to tell what you tell me."

50

"I don't know if that would work."

"Sure it would. . . . I've got a needle." Jenny opened her backpack and took out a tiny sewing kit.

Jenny is always ready for anything. Maybe it's because her father is a Boy Scout leader and the whole family takes the "Be Prepared" oath seriously.

I watched Jenny write her name on her folder, prick her finger, then smear her name with blood. It was gross. "Tell me," she said.

Her eyes nearly popped out when I told her about chugalugging beer. "What did your parents say?"

"I didn't tell them about the beer. They'd call Kim's father or Mr. Hansen or even the police. I told them about calling Daddy."

Just like Leo and Mom, Jenny yelled, "You called your father from Kim Adams's house!"

Two eighth graders walking in front of us turned around. "Shut up, Jenny." I didn't want the whole world to know.

"What did your father say?" she whispered.

"Nothing much. We didn't talk long."

"Are you going to call him again?"

"No. He called Mom on Sunday."

"This is better than the soaps. What happened?"

"He wants me to come to Florida, sometime soon. I guess my call shook him up or something."

"Are you going?"

"I don't know. Mom and Leo said it was up to me." I didn't want to tell Jenny how much I miss Daddy. Leo is a really good guy, but he's not my father.

"Do you want to go?"

I shrugged. "I guess so." It's a mess, I thought. I don't want to hurt Mom's and Leo's feelings. It would be a whole lot easier if they would just say, "You can't go."

When we got to school, Jenny poked me. "Oh, God, don't let me puke," I said. Kim, Stacey, Andrea, Patti, and Lisa were standing in front of the school. Somehow, my feet walked up the stairs.

"Nice sweater, Jenny," Patti said, giggling.

Jenny ignored them. They started clucking like chickens as I opened the front door. "Have you seen Richard?" Kim asked me in a sticky-sweet voice. "I have."

"Boy, they are really weird," said Jenny. "I'll see you at lunch."

I hurried to my locker. On it was a picture of a chicken. And underneath the picture was a sign.

ERIN MITCHELL LOVES RICHARD FRAIZER.

Nine

What happens if you drop dead in school? Do the paramedics come? Or do you go straight to one of those funeral places? I grabbed the ERIN LOVES RICHARD sign, stuffed it into my pocket, and looked around.

David Peters, Richard's best friend, was heading straight toward me. He's the only boy in sixth grade with a punk haircut and muscles.

"How's it going, Mitchell?" David asked, as he jabbed me in the arm.

I prayed he wouldn't see the chicken poster I was hiding in my social-studies book.

"Richard wants to know if it's true."

"If what is true?"

"You know." He punched me in the arm again. "The sign. Is it true? Or is it a joke?"

The bell rang and I was saved. "I've got to go. Mrs. Lewis kills if you're late," I said.

"I'll talk to you at lunch." David gave me another poke before he sprinted down the hall.

I took the chicken poster out of my social-studies book, threw it into the garbage, and raced to class. Mrs. Lewis was getting ready to take attendance. When she looked at me with her eyebrows in the up position, I knew I was in trouble.

"Absent yesterday, and almost tardy today, Erin. Do you have an admit slip?"

"Yes," I answered, wishing she'd hurry up and retire. Why does Mr. Hansen let somebody that old and crabby keep on teaching? Richard looked up and made a face like he was sucking on a lemon. We both got the giggles. Mrs. Lewis gave us the stare.

Jenny sent me a note which said, *What's going on?*

I mouthed the words, "I'll tell you at lunch."

At lunchtime, Jenny was waiting for me at the cafeteria door. She let out a scream when I told her what David Peters said. We almost got in trouble with the lunchroom ladies who are there to keep order. In line, Jenny and I were so busy talking I didn't see Ryan Williams, and bumped into him.

"Watch it," he growled, then grinned when he turned and saw me. My heart gave a funny little leap, which was weird, but then my whole life has been pretty weird lately.

"Have you memorized your poem for the poetry report?" Ryan asked.

"I haven't even decided on a poem."

"Pick a short one," Ryan said. "I did. Looney Lewis didn't say how long they have to be."

"All the poems I found were long. Really long."

"If you're going to the library on Saturday, I'll be there about one o'clock. I'll help you find a short poem."

"Okay," I answered.

"See ya Saturday, Mitchell."

He left me standing in line with my mouth open. Ryan Williams asked me out, and I said yes.

Jenny nudged me. "Move," she said. I concentrated on putting one foot in front of the other, and made it over to our table in the far corner of the cafeteria. I was glad Susie and Laurie were eating at another table. I had to talk to Jenny.

Before Jenny took a bite out of her hamburger, she said, "I think you're going to beat Kim Adams out of the popularity contest."

"Very funny," I said. "Ryan doesn't count."

"Why not?" asked Jenny. She poured ketchup onto her French fries. "He's not a nerd. He just goes his own way. He's different, but cute."

She sucked all the ketchup off a French fry and said, "Besides, he likes you."

"We're just friends."

"Whatever you say," Jenny answered, with a know-it-all smile. "But two boys are better than none. Tell me more about Richard."

Just as I was about to give her all the details, David Peters poked me in the back. My chocolate milk splashed on my jeans.

"Hey!" I yelled. "Cut it out."

"Richard wants to know," he said, tipping my chair back.

"I can't talk upside down," I said, trying to be cool even though I knew I had a chocolate-milk mustache and my knees were beginning to knock together.

David bumped my chair back.

"What about Richard and Kim?" I asked him.

"They broke up last week."

Now this was an interesting piece of news. Just as I was about to ask David for the details, the fire-alarm bell went off.

Every spring and fall, the fire alarm goes off at least once a week. It's part of the eighth-grade tradition. Last week, Mr. Hansen suspended two eighth graders for pulling the alarm. This week, he'll probably suspend the whole school. He looked so mad standing on the driveway, I thought the firemen would have to douse him with water. You could almost see the smoke coming out of his ears.

David and I got separated going back into school. For the rest of the day, my mind kept buzzing around what he said. "Richard wants to know."

Why? That was the three-million-dollar question. Could it be, *was* it possible? Did Richard Fraizer like me? It had to be a joke. But maybe it wasn't. Maybe that's why Kim was so mean to me. I almost felt sorry for her. Almost.

After school, Jenny was late getting to the corner. While I was waiting for her, I wrote Richard's name three different ways on my folder. I wrote *Mr. and Mrs. Richard Fraizer. Mrs. Richard Fraizer. Erin Fraizer.*

Then I wrote Ryan Williams's name and did the same thing. I looked at both names, Fraizer and Williams. It was almost as confusing as trying to decide between Mitchell and Zanin.

"Hey, Mitchell!" David Peters was across the street on his bike. "Where do you live?"

"444 Summerdale. Why?" He didn't answer. He just waved and rode off.

When Jenny finally got to the corner, I told her everything. "What am I going to do?"

"Beats me," said Jenny. "What do you want to do?"

"If I knew what to do, I wouldn't have to ask."

"Well, you don't have to get huffy." Jenny started to walk ahead.

"I'm sorry, Jen," I called.

She turned around and smiled. "I have an idea," she said.

When Jenny gets excited, she starts skipping around. She started skipping around the mailbox. "It's a great idea. We'll call a psychic."

"Jen-ny. Be serious. How do you know a psychic?"

Jenny's eyes were dancing. "I don't know one personally. But I know how to call one." She laughed.

I wanted to shake her. "Tell me." I could feel a fight coming on.

"Chill out," Jenny said, still laughing. "Amy brought home the *National Tattler* and there are ads for psychics on the back page. We can call one up. It'll be a blast."

"You're crazy, Jenny."

"Come on," she pleaded. "You can find out if Richard really likes you. And you can find out if Richard or Ryan is your true love."

I looked at Jenny. She wasn't kidding. Maybe she knew what she was talking about. Maybe a psychic could help me decide. Maybe she'd have the answers to all my questions.

When we got to Jenny's house, we started rummaging

through the pile of papers stacked on the family-room table till we found the *National Tattler*. Jenny read the ad. "Sister Lena guarantees help by phone. One question answered free. Immediate results. Call now. 312-555-0656."

"But I have more than one question."

"Put them all together."

"I want to know if Richard likes me. I'll ask another time about Mitchell or Zanin." I didn't want to push my luck.

Jenny handed me the telephone. "Go for it."

I started to push the buttons, but when I got to the last button, I chickened out. I hung up. "I better not call," I said. "Sister Lena could know who I am and send me a bill. Mom and Leo would kill me."

"Don't be dumb," Jenny said, picking up the telephone. "It says one question answered free."

"Are you sure?"

Jenny shoved the *National Tattler* under my nose. "Read it yourself."

I pushed the buttons again. "It's ringing," I whispered. Then I hung up.

"Give me the phone," said Jenny in a disgusted voice. She pushed the buttons. "Sister Lena," she said, trying to sound like her mother, "I'm calling for my free question."

I could tell Sister Lena was saying something and it

wasn't good. Jenny was twisting a strand of her hair into a tight curl.

"How do you know how old I am?" Jenny sputtered. She listened for a minute, then banged down the telephone.

"What did she say?"

Jenny flopped down on the sofa. "She said she was psychic, and she knew I wasn't twenty-one."

"Now what?"

"We'll think of something else."

I looked at the clock. "I've got to go. Mom will think I've been kidnapped."

Jenny walked me to the corner. "Call me tonight," I told her.

My brain started spinning again. Richard or Ryan kept tumbling around in my head like clothes in the washing machine.

Halfway down the street, I looked up and saw David and Richard circling their bikes. My legs started turning to jello. Maybe they're lost. Maybe they're looking for directions. I kept on walking. They kept circling their bikes until I reached the front steps.

Richard grinned at me and David zoomed up the sidewalk. "We're playing Jackson, Saturday," David said. "The game starts at one o'clock."

"Be there, Mitchell," said Richard as they rode off.

Ten

Saturday. It finally came. I looked at the clock. 9:30 A.M. Last time I had looked at the clock, it said 5:27 A.M. This had been the longest night of my life.

I made a flying leap out of bed and looked into the mirror. No zits. Jenny found one on her forehead Thursday and Susie had one on her chin yesterday. I was sure an enormous zit would be growing on my nose this morning. But my nose looked okay. Big as ever but not red and ugly.

I switched on the radio, picked up my teddy bear,

Fluffy, and danced around the room to the Crazy Kisses hit song, "Sweet Love."

"Erin." Mom was knocking at the door. "Turn down that radio!" she shouted. "Jenny is on the telephone."

Mom was wearing a frown when I opened the door. She's been a crab all week. I guess her back hurts. The doctor said the twins were pressing on a nerve. It sounded gross.

I picked up the upstairs telephone. "I can't go to the game with you," Jenny said. "I'm grounded."

"What did you do?"

"I eavesdropped on Amy's conversation with her new boyfriend. I just wanted to pick up a tip or two. But my dad caught me. Boy, was he mad. He said eavesdropping was just like stealing. I can't go to the game with you. I'm sorry."

"What if Kim and Andrea show up? I'll be by myself."

"Don't be a dork. You'll be with Richard. He told you to be there."

"What if he was just joking around?"

"It didn't sound like a joke to me," Jenny said. Then she asked, "What did Ryan say when you called him? Was he mad?"

"I didn't call him."

"Why not?" Jenny yelled.

I felt like a bomb went off in my ear. "I didn't have time," I told her. "When I got home, Mom and Leo were

going out for dinner. They were in a rotten mood. I had
to go over to Catherine's."

"Catherine would have let you call."

Jenny can be a real rag. Sometimes she reminds me
of Lincoln sniffing out a bone. She just never gives
up.

"Catherine and I played the piano and baked chocolate-chip cookies after supper. I never had a chance to
call him."

"Are you going to call him now?"

"I guess so."

"I have to go," Jenny whispered. "My dad is coming
up the stairs." She hung up.

I put down the telephone and looked up Ryan's number. The line was busy. What if he waits all afternoon at
the library? What if he shows up at the game? Why didn't
I tell him in school? My stomach tied itself into little
knots thinking about Ryan.

When I walked into the kitchen, I knew something
was wrong. Leo was wearing his bathrobe, and he always
gets dressed for breakfast. Mom kept staring at her coffee
cup.

Leo said, "Sit down, Erin. Your mother and I want to
talk to you."

Now what? It must be something pretty awful if we're
having a meeting before breakfast. "What did I do?" I
asked, trying to remember what I did wrong. Maybe Mom

heard me talking about Ryan. She'd have a complete fit if she knew I didn't tell him I wasn't going to the library. But Mom wouldn't eavesdrop.

Maybe she found the books Jenny and I bought a couple of weeks ago, *Promise of Passion* and *Surrender*. I hid them in the bottom of my jeans drawer under my diary.

"You didn't do anything, punkin," Leo said.

"Your father called Wednesday," Mom said. I watched her swallow hard when she said "your father." "He wants you to visit him soon."

Now I knew why Mom looked so mad the past few days. Maybe that's why they went out for dinner last night and didn't ask me. We usually go to Dino's for pizza on Friday nights.

"Why didn't you tell me?" I nearly shouted at Mom.

"Your mother and I wanted to talk things over before we told you," Leo said, rubbing his bald spot.

"When does he want me to come?" I managed to ask. I couldn't believe it. Daddy wanted me to visit him. It was too much. I was happy. I was scared. I wasn't sure I was ready to go.

"Your father," Mom said slowly, in a funny voice, "thinks Memorial Day weekend would be a good time." She handed me a white envelope.

It was a letter to Mom and Leo from Daddy. Before I read it, I walked over to the calendar. "Memorial Day is next week." I felt cold prickles on my neck. Everything was happening too fast.

I started reading Daddy's letter. It said:

Dear Kate and Leo,

As you know, Florida will be my home base until the middle of June. I hope you have given our telephone conversation more thought. I really would like a chance to be with Erin, and I think she deserves a chance to know me.

I'm hoping Memorial Day weekend will work out for her. I have enclosed an open-ended round-trip ticket, just in case. I'll call Erin on Saturday.

As ever,

Paul

P.S. Congratulations on the twins. Erin told me your good news.

Mom and Leo were watching me. I put the letter down on the kitchen table. It was so quiet, I could hear Lincoln breathing. He sighed and so did I.

"Should I go?" I asked.

Mom answered slowly, like syrup dripping out of a bottle. "It's up to you, Erin."

Parents are weird. When Jenny and I wanted to see *Dance of Death*, Mom and Leo had a major fit. And Mom made me wash off the tawny brown eye shadow I tried on last week. How come flying off to Florida to see Daddy, who's practically a stranger, is up to me?

I don't know what to do. If I go, Mom and Leo will pretend it's okay, but they'll have sad eyes. And if I don't go, maybe I'll never have another chance to see Daddy. He could get lost in Africa or marry a movie star who hates kids.

Why do I have to choose? Kids shouldn't have to choose between parents.

I couldn't stay in the kitchen anymore. "I've got to get ready for the game," I said, trying not to sniffle.

"Erin, we have to talk," Mom said.

I heard Leo say, "Let her go, Kate," as I ran out of the room.

In my room, I took Daddy's picture off my desk. "Why did you leave?" I asked him. "You got me into this mess. What am I going to do?"

Daddy's picture didn't have the answer. I put it face-down on the dresser and looked into the mirror. Ugh. What a disaster. My eyes were red and watery. I stared at myself for a while. "What are you going to do, dummy?" I asked myself. I shrugged and stuck out my tongue at my reflection. I didn't have the answer.

Maybe Catherine could help. Maybe the tea leaves had the answer. "I'm going over to Catherine's," I called, running out the front door. Mom and Leo were still in the kitchen.

Catherine was planting seeds in her garden. I think she has one of the prettiest gardens in Lilac Grove.

"I was hoping you'd come over this morning," Catherine said. "I made blueberry muffins just in case. Help me finish the planting and then I'll make some tea." Catherine handed me a package of zinnia seeds.

I planted the seeds carefully. The earth felt good, soft and warm. I watched a honeybee land on a tulip.

"Flowers are lucky," I said.

Catherine smiled at me and asked, "Why do you think so?"

I shrugged. "I don't know. I guess because they don't have to decide what kind of flower to be." I scattered the rest of the zinnia seeds in the row I had dug for them. "While the zinnias are growing, they aren't worrying if they should be tulips or marigolds."

Catherine came over to me and put her arm across my shoulders.

"It stinks," I blurted out.

"What stinks?" Catherine asked, pulling me closer.

"Divorce."

"Want to talk about it?"

I shook my head, *no*.

"How about some blueberry muffins?"

The muffins tasted so good I ate three of them. When I finished my tea, I peered into the cup.

"What are you looking for?" Catherine asked.

"A message, I guess." I told Catherine about the letter from Daddy. "I don't know what to do about anything."

Catherine looked at me with her chin resting on her hands. Her dark blue eyes almost looked black. "The tea leaves don't have the answer, pet. You do."

"I do? Where?"

Catherine pointed to the middle of my chest. "It's right inside of you."

"I can't find it."

"You will," she said.

How did she know, I wondered.

Eleven

"Get off." I poked Lincoln, who had snuggled down on my bed. "Mom will yell." I thought she might yell when I got back from Catherine's, but she didn't. All she said was, straighten your room before you go to the game.

Leo handed me a stack of towels to take upstairs. They didn't mention Daddy. I don't know why.

I started making my bed. I smoothed the wrinkles out of my comforter. I used to have a brown-and-white spread, but when we decorated my room, Mom and I picked out a white comforter with red roses. It's neat

69

sleeping on a bed of roses. I wondered what kind of bed I'd have in Florida, if I decided to go.

Maybe Daddy has a room waiting for me. I'd miss my room here. It's perfect. Leo mixed pink and white paint and it turned out just right. Mom called it pale pink carnation. We bought my bed at an auction. That was fun but scary. I thought for sure the fat lady with the horn-rimmed glasses was going to buy my bed. But Leo kept raising his fingers and we won.

I flopped down on my bed and buried my nose in my comforter. I wondered what it would be like to have two beds. I'd be a two-bed kid like Matt Anderson, Ryan's best friend. His mother and father are divorced, too. They share Matt. He's supposed to feel at home in both houses, so he has two of everything. Two fathers. Two toothbrushes and two sets of rules. Matt doesn't have to worry about two names, though. He gets to stay an Anderson.

Mom and Leo won't keep the adoption on hold forever. I'll have to decide sometime. I got up and took my lucky penny off the dresser. Maybe it has all the answers to my questions.

"Heads," I called and flipped it. It turned up tails. That means I'm not supposed to go to Florida. Leo and Mom will be glad. Maybe they're afraid I'll stay in Florida forever.

I rubbed the penny again. "Tails," I called. It came up heads. That means I change my name to Zanin.

I flipped it three more times. Each time I had a different answer. "None of them count," I shouted, putting my penny in the bottom of my pajama drawer.

"Erin," Mom was calling me. "Your father is on the telephone."

I stumbled over Lincoln getting to the door. "What should I tell him?" I whispered to Mom.

Mom sighed and covered the telephone with her hand. "It's okay for you to go," she said. "But remember, you don't have to go."

"I don't know what to do," I said, feeling very dumb. "I can't make up my mind."

"Your father wants to know." Mom handed me the telephone. "You have to decide, Erin." I could tell she was losing her patience by the way she was tapping her foot.

"Hi, Erin," Daddy said. His voice always sounds nice. Quiet and deep. "I'm looking forward to your visit. We have a lot of catching up to do."

I didn't say anything because I didn't know what to say.

"You're coming, aren't you?" Daddy asked.

I still didn't say anything. I kept rubbing the back of my shoe against my leg. Daddy's voice sounded higher when he said, "Erin, aren't you going to come?"

"I'll come," I said. My stomach took a flying leap into my throat. I didn't know I was going to say yes.

"Good," Daddy said. I could hear the smile in his voice. "I'll pick you up at the airport. Okay?"

"Okay." It still didn't seem real. Maybe I was in the middle of a dream.

"We'll have a great time. Better let me talk to your mom. See you next week."

I handed Mom the telephone and raced for the bathroom. Barfing on the floor would be so gross. I made it, just in time. Three blueberry muffins are too many blueberry muffins.

I washed my face and brushed my teeth, twice. I was afraid to look in the mirror, but I did. Awful. I looked just awful, pale and droopy. The game was in half an hour. How could I let Richard see me looking like I fell into the flour canister?

Mom's mascara was on the shelf. I gave my eyelashes a quick coat, then I smeared her Desert Pink blush on my cheeks. I didn't want to use her brush. Makeup brushes are as personal as toothbrushes. At least that's what it said in *Beautiful You*.

Mom was still talking to Daddy when I came out of the bathroom. "I'm going to the game," I said running by her, hoping she wouldn't see any makeup on my face.

"Are you okay?" Mom asked, holding the telephone away from her ear. "Your cheeks looked flushed."

"I'm fine, Mom. I've got to hurry. I'll be late," I answered. I couldn't be late. What if Richard thought I wasn't coming?

My bike was in the garage and the front tire was almost flat. Great. It was a good thing Leo bought me a bicycle pump last year.

Please let Richard be there. Please let him talk to me, I thought as I pumped up the tire. *Please don't let it be a joke. Please, God, please, please.* I crossed my fingers as I rode along, just in case God was busy.

No one was around when I passed Jenny's house. Why did she have to be grounded today? What if Kim and Andrea show up at the game? Shut up, I said to myself. I wasn't going back home.

As I rode past the library, I saw Ryan's bike in the rack. I knew it was his bike because it was plastered with Cubs baseball stickers.

I looked at my watch. It was one o'clock. I was supposed to meet Richard now. I stopped riding and stared at the library. One part of me wanted to run in and tell Ryan I was going to the game and the other part of me wanted to just ride on by. I locked my bike in the rack and went into the library.

Ryan was sitting on the floor in the Science Fiction section. He was wearing his Cubs baseball hat and his *Go Bears Go* sweatshirt. He's a real fan.

Ryan looked up at me and grinned. When he gets rid

of his braces, he'll probably have a nice smile. "I'm taking notes for my next Sherlock Holmes story," he said. "Sherlock and Watson are going to the moon."

Ryan is always writing stories and Mrs. Lewis is always yelling at him to "Get down to business."

"Did you find a poem yet?" Ryan asked. "I'm doing 'Stringbean Small' by Jack Prelutsky. It's about a basketball player and it's only eight lines. I found it in a great book, *The New Kid On The Block*.

"I haven't found one yet," I told him. "They're all too long."

"Here," Ryan said. He handed me *Where The Sidewalk Ends*. "They're short and funny."

"Thanks. Maybe I'll check it out," I said. "I have to go."

"You do? Okay. Pick out a funny poem." Ryan grinned. "We need all the laughs we can get in Looney Lewis's class."

I walked out of the library feeling funny. Why did I want Ryan to care whether or not I stayed?

I rode my bike as fast as I could to the park.

Twelve

Everyone was there. Richard, David, and Kim were standing near home plate. Kim looked perfect. She was wearing blue paisley pants, a white polo shirt, and gold hoop earrings.

Why did I wear jeans and a red sweatshirt? Richard would never notice me.

Andrea, Lisa, Patti, and Stacey ran over to Kim. They saw me, poked Kim, and started giggling. I felt prickly all over. It's hard to be alone in a big group. It's worse than being alone by yourself. Why did Jenny have to go and get herself grounded?

I looked around hoping somebody, anybody would talk to me. All right! I saw Matt Anderson, Laurie Conto, and Susie McKenna circling their bikes near second base.

"Where's Jenny?" Laurie asked.

"Grounded," I told her.

"What a drag," Laurie said. "I came close to being grounded once, but my mom couldn't stand me crying. She said she was the one being punished."

"Ow!" I felt a punch in my right shoulder. David and Richard were behind me. Richard looked so good in his number-thirteen jersey.

"How's it going, Mitchell?" Richard asked me.

"Okay," I answered. Then I didn't know what to say. My dream had come true. Richard Fraizer was standing next to me, talking to me, and I couldn't think of a thing to say.

"Play ball!" the umpire yelled.

"See ya, Mitchell," Richard said.

"Good luck," I called.

"Thanks," he yelled over his shoulder.

It was true, hearts can go pitter-patter because mine was. Maybe he does like me, a little bit, anyway.

I turned around to see if Kim was watching. She was. But I didn't care. I gave her my best smile and looked away. Why couldn't Jenny be here?

Laurie grabbed my arm. "Isn't he awesome?" she asked, as Richard came up to bat.

76

I hoped Laurie couldn't tell how much I liked Richard. I didn't take my eyes off him for the rest of the game. I wondered how many of the sixth-grade girls were in love with him. Probably everyone but Jenny. She's always in love with her sister Amy's boyfriends.

When Richard came up to bat in the ninth inning, the game was tied four to four. Richard swung.

"Foul ball," the umpire called.

We all held our breath. Richard swung again. *Crack.* He raced around the bases. A home run.

Laurie, Susie, and I started yelling. Matt Anderson punched our shoulders. Ryan rode his bike onto the field. "We won! We won!" everyone yelled.

"Hi, Mitchell," Ryan said. He didn't seem surprised to see me. I answered him, but I was trying to see where Richard was going.

Kim was heading toward him. Stacey, Andrea, Lisa, and Patti followed her like ducklings following their mother. Everybody crowded around Richard. Andrea waved to David and the rest of the team. They all ran over to where Kim and Richard were standing. Kim was talking to Richard. It looked like she didn't have any trouble knowing what to say.

I felt like a little kid watching her balloon float away.

David Peters turned around and headed back toward us. "Going to Kim's?" he asked. "She's ordering pizza for everybody."

I shook my head and answered no.

" 'Miss Stuck-Up' didn't ask us," Matt Anderson said.

"Oh. Okay. See ya around, Mitchell." David took off.

"Let's hit Dairy Delight," Ryan said.

All the way to Dairy Delight, there was a funny hollow feeling in my chest. I kept thinking *Richard loves Kim, Richard loves Kim.*

Ryan bought me a caramel turtle again. I tried to give him the money, but he wouldn't take it. The caramel turtle tasted pretty good. Almost as good as the first one.

When we got to my house, Ryan put his bike on the grass and we sat on the front steps. "Want some lemonade?" I asked him. Caramel turtles make you thirsty.

We sipped lemonade from paper cups and Lincoln came out and sniffed Ryan. I guess Ryan passed the sniff test because Lincoln licked his hand. Sitting with Ryan, the hollow place in my chest disappeared. We talked about school, Mrs. Lewis, and pizza. Ryan hates mushrooms, too. We both like double cheese with sausage and onions.

Then we started talking about vacations. Ryan's been to California, Maine, and Florida. He's been to Florida twice. I told him about visiting Daddy.

"Were you scared, the first time you flew?" I asked him.

Ryan grinned and scratched Lincoln's ear. "Maybe a little."

"Well, I'm scared a lot," I said, surprising myself.

"It's no big deal," said Ryan. "When we went to Florida the last time, there was a kid travelling alone. The flight attendant took him up to the cockpit." Ryan picked up his bike. "Maybe you'll get to go up front, too."

Just thinking about being in the cockpit of a plane made my stomach twitch. How could the pilot keep track of all those blinking lights? And what if he started talking to me and steered the wrong way? It would be all my fault if the plane crashed.

"I'll stay in my seat," I told Ryan. "I might get lost."

Ryan laughed. "I have to get going," he said. "Remember, you risk your life every time you walk into Looney Lewis's class, so flying should be easy."

Thirteen

The plane flew through the clouds. I looked out the window and watched a wing drop into the ocean. I grabbed for it and fell out of the plane.

"Help!" I yelled, flapping my arms, trying to fly. "Help!"

Mom and Leo came running into my room. They sat down on my bed. I snuggled in close, as close to Mom as I could get. She's getting pretty big, so it's hard to get as close as I used to.

"You were dreaming, Erin." Mom ran her hand down

my cheek. She used to do that when I was a little kid. It felt good.

I didn't want to tell Mom and Leo I dreamed the plane crashed, it might scare them. After they tucked me back into bed, I still couldn't sleep, so I turned on the radio. B96 was playing an hour of hits. I fell asleep listening to Crazy Kisses' new song, "I'll Find You, Baby."

I don't know why, but I woke up thinking about sunglasses. Mine are old and make me look like a bug. Jenny has mirrored ones. I jumped out of bed and called her. "Are you wearing your sunglasses tomorrow?"

"I don't know. I might. Why? Do you want to borrow them?" Jenny always gets right to the point.

"Could I take them to Florida?" I crossed my fingers and hoped she'd say yes. She did. "Thanks, Jenny, I promise not to lose them."

"You do and you die." Jenny giggled. "Amy's new boyfriend, Jeff, thinks I look cool in them. They go with everything. What are you going to wear on the plane?"

"My new jeans. Mom wanted me to wear a skirt, but I talked her out of it."

"I can't believe you're leaving tonight. It's just like a soap opera."

Back in my room, I checked out my stuff. Mom had packed my swimsuit, beach coat, and shorts.

"I'll see you tonight," I whispered to Daddy's picture.

Boy, did that sound weird. Six years is a long time between visits.

David Peters was standing in front of my locker when I got to school. I wondered why. He and Richard had been hanging around Kim all week. They acted as if I were invisible.

"Richard wants to know if you're going to the game tonight."

"I can't, I'll be on an airplane," I answered.

"Don't be funny, Mitchell. Richard wants to know."

"I'm not being funny. Did Richard have another fight with Kim?"

"So what if he did. He wants you to be at the game."

"Tell Richard I can't go to the game. I'm going to Florida."

"Tell him yourself." David took off down the hall as the warning bell rang.

While I was straightening out my books which were falling out of my locker, I saw the note. It said, *Stay away from Richard or else.*

I knew it was from Kim. At lunch, I showed it to Jenny. She laughed.

"It's not funny, Jenny." I put down my hot dog. "What if Kim hires someone to beat me up? What should I do?"

"Show the note to Richard."

"Are you crazy? Kim would kill me."

Jenny shook her head and grabbed some of my French fries. "She's scared of you."

"Me? Why would she be scared of me?"

Jenny finished my fries. "Richard must like you a little. I saw him watching you when you gave your poetry report. And he's always sending David Peters to talk to you."

"It doesn't mean anything." How could it? Richard likes Kim and everyone knows it. He'll never like me or look at me the way he looks at Kim. Probably no one ever will. I wanted to tear Kim's note into little pieces and put it on her desk, but I put it in my pocket instead.

Jenny reached into her purse and handed me her sunglasses. "Try them on," she said.

"Not here. I'd feel silly."

"Don't be a dork. Put them on," Jenny persisted.

"How do I look?"

"You look cool, dude. Remember that. And forget about Kim. She'll trip over her own feet one of these days."

Kim sailed into class looking as cool as ever in white painter's paints and red hoop earrings. I watched Richard watching her. He smiled at me, too. I smiled back, hoping Kim wasn't watching me. I could feel her note in my pocket.

Everyone laughed when Ryan gave his report on "Stringbean Small." Even Mrs. Lewis's lips quivered at the corners when he bowed at the end of the poem.

Ryan walked out of class with me. "When's the big flight?" he asked.

"Tonight," I told him.

"Are you still scared?" he asked.

"Sort of. I guess."

Ryan put his hand in his pocket and pulled out a small package and handed it to me. "Here," he said. My face must have looked funny because Ryan laughed and said, "It's not a joke. Open it."

Why did Ryan give me two packages of Double Bubble and Juicy Fruit?

"Your ears won't pop if you keep on chewing," he said. "And take this, too."

Ryan's face started turning pink as he handed me his picture.

"Thanks, Ryan," I said. Ryan Williams is the weirdest boy I know, a nice weird, though.

"See ya, Mitchell." Ryan grinned and gave my arm a quick jab.

I put Ryan's picture and the gum into my jeans pocket. "I'll send you a postcard," I called after him as he ran down the hall.

Then I took Kim's note out of my other pocket, tore it into little pieces, and threw it into the trash.

Fourteen

"Erin, I have something for you." Catherine was standing on her front porch. I ran over.

"First a hug." Catherine opened her arms and I snuggled against her. She smelled good. Her perfume reminded me of spice cake and Christmas trees. She kissed the top of my head.

"Now," Catherine said, "take this with you. It's fun to read." She handed me a small blue paperback called *A Sky Filled With Poems*.

"Thanks." I hugged Catherine, gave her a quick kiss, and hurried down the stairs.

Mom and Leo were waiting in the car. All the way to O'Hare Airport Mom fussed. "Remember," she said, "put on the sunscreen I packed for you before you go out in the sun. And wear the hat I packed for you."

"M-o-m, I can't wear a hat. I'll look like a dorky little kid."

Mom didn't listen, she just kept rattling off orders. "Don't swim alone. Call as soon as the plane lands. Tell the flight attendant if you don't feel well."

I listened with my ears, but not my head. The thoughts in my head were racing. What if Daddy wasn't at the airport? What if he was there and didn't recognize me? Last night, on the telephone, he said he'd be waiting at the gate. I told him I'd be wearing a blue-and-white-striped blouse and jeans. "My hair is short, dark, and curly," I said to him. "Just like Mom's." Then I realized what I had said. I wanted to grab the words and shove them back into my mouth.

"I'll recognize you right away," Daddy said in a reassuring voice. But what if he didn't? My stomach started taking nosedives just thinking about it, so I flipped through Catherine's book.

Then I checked out my purse. I had Mom and Leo's picture, Jenny's sunglasses, her picture, Ryan's picture, his gum, traveller's checks, silver-blue eye shadow that Jenny and I bought yesterday (Daddy might let me wear it), and my lucky penny. I wondered if it was going to

86

take more than my lucky penny to get me to Florida and back.

Mom held on to my hand while Leo went up to the desk to check me in. I guess she was feeling scared about my going. She looked as white as her dusting powder. When Leo came back and said, "All set," I kissed them good-bye.

A dark-haired flight attendant showed me to my seat in the plane. I was glad because the aisles were crowded and the numbers were confusing. My seat was a window seat in the nonsmoking section near the exit sign. I snapped the seat belt across my stomach, then I looked into the pocket of the seat in front of me. The barf bag was there. I'd die if I had to use it, but at least it was there, just in case.

I popped Ryan's Double Bubble in my mouth and looked around. I didn't see any kids my age, just babies. A man wearing two gold earrings in the same ear sat across the aisle from me. I tried to picture Leo wearing an earring. It made me giggle. I wondered if Daddy wore an earring. It's hard not knowing what your father is really like. I concentrated on blowing bubbles.

A tall, thin lady wearing a bright green pants suit with a matching scarf on her head sat down next to me. She stared at the double bubble I was blowing. I tried not to stare back, but she looked like a lime popsicle. I could tell she didn't like kids. She didn't smile or ask me my name. She just took a fat book out of her green purse and started to read.

When the "Fasten your seat belt" sign went on, I knew we were ready for takeoff. Mom and Leo had explained what to expect. The plane started to move. My stomach. It jumped right into my throat. *Please, God, don't let me barf.* Everybody on the plane, especially the lady in green would smell it and hate me. It would be as bad as the time I threw up in third grade and Miss Wilson had to open all the windows in the classroom. You can't open windows in an airplane.

We're rolling. My heart was pounding. I wanted to yell, *Stop the plane!*

I looked over at the lady in green. She was holding on to the arms of the seat. She gave me a funny little smile.

I smiled back. "It's my first time on a plane," I said.

"Mine, too." She licked her lips.

"Do you want some gum? Your ears won't pop if you chew." I gave her a half-stick of Double Bubble. We both chewed our gum. I chewed so hard, I bit the inside of my mouth.

"I guess we made it," the lady in green said with a sigh as the "No Smoking" sign went off. She opened her book and started to read again. I was glad she didn't want to talk. She could have been the kind of person who asks you your whole life history, just because you're a kid.

After a while, the dark-haired flight attendant brought

dinner in little plastic plates. There was a fruit cup, not bad, but it had only one cherry, stew, and chocolate cake. The stew had peas in it. Ugh. Peas are the worst vegetable, well, almost the worst, brussels sprouts are the absolute worst.

The chocolate cake was good but too small. I ate every last crumb. The lady in green asked me if I wanted her cake, but I said "No, thank you." I didn't want her to think I was a pig.

I didn't have anything to drink because then I'd have to go to the bathroom for sure. The thought of going to the bathroom in an airplane made me nervous. What if a man came in while I was there, I'd die. Or what if I locked myself in and couldn't get out? You can't call the fire department when you're flying over Tennessee.

I closed my eyes and tried to think about other things for the rest of the flight. I thought about Mom, Leo, Catherine, Richard, Ryan, Jenny, and Lincoln. I wondered what they were doing, if they missed me.

While I was thinking, the pilot announced we were flying over the ocean and we'd be landing in twelve minutes. Twelve minutes? Twelve more minutes until I would see Daddy. What if he didn't know me? What if he thought I was an ugly kid?

I grabbed my brush out of my purse and ran it through my hair. Maybe the silver-blue eye shadow would help, I thought. No. I might smear it. Sunglasses. Jenny's sunglasses. I dug down to the bottom of my purse and found them. Yesterday, when I tried them on, Jenny had said, "Cool, dude, very cool."

Next, my ears started popping. I crammed two sticks of Double Bubble into my mouth. The lady in green took a stick of Juicy Fruit.

I took my lucky penny out of my purse and held on to it until the plane bumped down on the runway. I was really scared. I didn't know anybody in West Palm Beach, Florida. What if Daddy wasn't waiting at the gate?

Fifteen

The dark-haired flight attendant walked down the ramp with me. "I'll tell the gate agent your father is meeting you," she said.

The gate agent smiled when he saw me, but it wasn't a real smile. "Stand over here." He pointed to the ticket counter.

I didn't see Daddy anywhere. Where was he? My heart jumped when I saw a tall man with a beard heading toward me, but it wasn't Daddy. Why wasn't he here? He *promised*. My hands started to sweat. My mind started racing. If he didn't come, I could call Mom and

Leo. No. They'd flip out. I could call Daddy. Maybe he mixed up the days. Or maybe he had an accident. What if he was lying in a ditch somewhere?

Why wasn't he here?

The lady in green turned around, waved good-bye, and walked away.

I kept looking at everyone. No one noticed me. I will not cry, I thought, pressing my lips together, hard. Where was he? Where was Daddy? Why wasn't he here?

"Erin, Erin, over here." A tall man wearing jeans and a blue-and-white sports shirt was waving at me.

"Daddy, Daddy!" I cried.

He opened his arms and I ran into them. Daddy kissed me and I kissed him back. "Let me look at you," he said. His voice was low and husky as if he had a bad cold.

"You're all grown-up, Erin," Daddy said. "And beautiful." He put his arm around my shoulder and gave me a squeeze.

I leaned against Daddy. I wanted to stay there close to him forever. Being with him was like all my Christmas mornings tied up in one big present. And best of all, I didn't have to go up to him and say, "Excuse me, I'm your daughter."

"Come on." Daddy smiled at me. "We'll get your suitcase."

I told him I had to call Mom and Leo. "Sure," he said.

When Daddy put my suitcase in his car, he said, "Hope

you're not too tired to stop for a bite to eat. I thought we'd go for spaghetti or something."

Food. How was I going to eat? I could feel the airplane stew sloshing around in my stomach. "Okay," I answered. Maybe I could order the kid-size plate.

The restaurant was small. Green-and-red lights blinked around the windows. We sat at a table with a red-and-white-checkered cloth. I ordered spaghetti and a Coke. Daddy ordered Eggplant Parmigiana. It was freaky. Daddy likes the same kind of food Leo does.

"How's school?" Daddy asked.

"Okay." I took small sips of my Coke.

"What's your favorite subject?"

"Gym."

Daddy laughed. "It was my favorite subject, too," he said. "What's your favorite sport?"

I told him basketball. I wanted to tell him about the time I made the winning basket when we played the seventh grade, but I felt funny. He might think I was showing off.

There were a million questions I wanted to ask him. Where are you going next? Do you have a girlfriend? Do you really love me? What kind of pizza do you like? Why did you say it was okay for me to change my name? Instead, I picked at my spaghetti. Daddy didn't seem to notice. He was making little figures out of the extra straws.

I was glad he turned on the tape deck when we got into his car. I was too tired to talk anymore. The music was soft and dreamy. Daddy said it was called "Songs of the Seashore." It made me sleepy, so I closed my eyes. It was almost dark when we pulled into a garage. Daddy came around and opened the car door for me.

"Is this a hotel?" There were real flowers in a red-and-gold vase sitting on a shiny round table in the lobby. I tried not to stare at the short man wearing a blue-and-gold uniform.

"It's a condominium complex," Daddy answered. "I stay here when I'm in Florida."

I followed Daddy to the elevator. I wished Jenny was with me. She'd think this place was awesome. I did, too. Inside the apartment, Daddy said, "Here's your room."

My room. At Daddy's. In Florida. Weird. Really weird. I sat down on a beige-and-white couch which was going to be my bed and looked around. I had my own stereo, telephone, bathroom, and TV. When I peeked through the blinds, I could see the ocean.

It took me a while to recognize the kid in the picture that was hanging over the couch. It was me, when I was six, the year Daddy left. I remembered the red dress and Mom putting my hair in ponytails.

I found all the school pictures I had sent Daddy under the glass on his desk. Seeing myself change from year to year gave me a funny feeling. My second-grade picture was the worst. My hair was a mess. I wouldn't let Mom brush it and my front tooth was missing. I looked like a Halloween witch.

When Daddy came into my room to say good night, I asked where he found the picture of me that was hanging on the wall.

"I didn't find it, Erin," Daddy said. "I had it with me when I left for California."

"You couldn't carry that big a picture on your motorcycle."

"You're right." Daddy laughed. "I had your school picture with me. Now that I have a home base, I had that picture blown up."

"I don't look like that anymore."

"No," Daddy said slowly. "No, you don't."

I didn't know what to say then.

Daddy said, "I'm glad you came, Erin. Maybe you'll let me take some new pictures before you leave."

I think Daddy wanted to kiss me good night but he didn't, he just said, "Sleep tight." I wanted to kiss him but I couldn't. I felt shy.

Daddy said I could call Mom and Leo, so I did. They sounded far away. It felt funny saying good night over the telephone. I missed Mom's three kisses.

My eyes popped open at 3:24. I turned over and peeked through the blinds. A light was blinking far out on the ocean. I wondered what it was, maybe a ship. I watched the light and the clock blink until 4:24. Then I got up. Maybe Daddy had some milk in the refrigerator.

When I walked into the kitchen, Daddy was sitting at the table watching the same light I had been watching. He patted a chair and asked, "Want some milk and cookies? I have oatmeal and chocolate chip."

"Chocolate chip," I said. We sat at the table munching cookies and drinking milk until the sky turned pink.

He told me how he's taking pictures of some of the places that are disappearing, like the rainforests in South America and the Everglades in Florida. I told him about being the tallest person in my class until Richard, Ryan, and Jenny caught up to me.

I made Daddy laugh when I told him about Jenny and me calling Sister Lena to help me decide between Richard and Ryan. I didn't tell him I thought about asking her which name I should choose, Mitchell or Zanin. I wanted to ask him the big question, why did he say it was all right for me to change my name to Zanin, but I couldn't.

For the next two days, Daddy and I swam, looked for turtle tracks on the beach, and took a drive to Sea World. Daddy introduced me to Windy, one of the dolphins. He's taking pictures of her for a kids' book. Everywhere we went, Daddy would take pictures of me. Sometimes my lips got stiff from smiling.

Sixteen

What a dream. Ryan and Richard were fighting over me. The weirdest part of the dream was that Ryan won. And then he kissed me in front of Jenny, Kim Adams, Andrea, and Mrs. Lewis. Part of me wanted to die and the other part wanted him to kiss me again. If real kissing is like dream kissing, it might not be too bad. I wondered what it would be like if Richard kissed me. I kissed my pillow just to practice. Blah. Pillow kissing isn't as good as dream kissing.

Maybe my dream would come true, someday. I

couldn't decide if it was Richard or Ryan I wanted to kiss me. Could you want both of them to kiss you? It was all pretty confusing.

When I walked into the kitchen, Daddy was cutting up a cantaloupe. "Want some melon?" he asked.

"Okay," I answered. I never eat it at home, but it tasted different here.

After breakfast, Daddy and I made plans for the day, souvenir shopping, a beach walk, and swimming. Neither one of us mentioned that today was my last day.

Time is funny. Four days can be longer than four years when you're waiting for Christmas. Or it can be the shortest four days of your life if you're staying with your father and wishing you were really talking.

I wanted to ask Daddy why he said I could change my name. But I couldn't, so I asked him about mailing my postcards instead. When I showed them to him, he asked, "Is Ryan someone special?"

"We're just friends." I pulled on the loose thread on my shorts and felt my face grow hot.

"It's hard to believe you're old enough to have a boyfriend," Daddy said.

"I don't have a boyfriend." I jumped up from the table. I felt totally confused. Why was Daddy looking at me with the same look Lincoln gets when he knows you're going out and he has to stay in the kitchen?

He caught my hand. "Hey, it's okay if you do have a boyfriend. I remember having a girlfriend when I was in sixth grade. Her name was Ingeborg Smith."

"Oh, Daddy." I giggled. It was hard to imagine Daddy being my age and having a girlfriend.

After we cleaned up the kitchen, Daddy and I drove to the shopping mall. He didn't say anything about my wearing silver-blue eye shadow. Maybe he couldn't tell because I was wearing Jenny's sunglasses.

At the mall, I picked out a blue-and-white Florida Beach Bunny sweatshirt for Jenny. Daddy bought the same one for me. I found a rubber steak for Lincoln, but I couldn't find anything for Mom, Leo, or Catherine. I knew they wouldn't want a plate that said *I Love Florida* or a plastic sea gull sitting on a perch. Daddy suggested seashells. He said we could look along the beach after lunch.

No one was on the beach when we came down. I guess they were afraid it might storm. Black clouds swirled around over the ocean and waves crashed and roared onto the beach. Daddy said he could smell the storm coming in, but we still had time to look for seashells.

We stopped and watched the sand crabs running sideways. They are really funny-looking creatures with big heads and long pincers. I wonder how they ever get where they're going.

We walked along the shore close to the waves but

couldn't find any shells. "There's always some at the cove," Daddy said. "Race you!"

I started running along the beach, close to the waves. Daddy was ahead of me. I was really sprinting along, trying to beat Daddy, not paying any attention to the waves, when a monster one rolled in.

I didn't see it coming and it knocked me down. Jenny's sunglasses went flying out of my beach-coat pocket. I tried to get up, but the waves kept knocking me down. "Daddy, help!" I yelled. Then I really got scared. Another monster wave swept over me. I felt like I had swallowed the ocean.

Don't let me die. Please don't let me die. The waves kept pushing me down. I lifted my head a little. Daddy was yelling, "I'm coming, Erin, I'm coming." He scooped me up. "Are you okay?" he asked in a shaky voice.

I nodded yes. I guess I was, but I couldn't stop shivering. "I lost Jenny's sunglasses," I cried.

"Better the sunglasses than you." Daddy hugged me tight.

He drew me a hot bath and I sat and soaked for a long time. The hot water felt so good. When I climbed out, I put on Daddy's thick, dark blue terry-cloth bathrobe and brushed my hair.

"Feeling better?" Daddy handed me a cup of steaming chicken broth. I curled up beside him on the couch and sipped the broth.

I still felt shaky inside. And I had that awful hollow feeling in my chest again. My head was all mixed-up. How can you want to be two places at once? It was warm and cozy sitting next to Daddy, but I wanted Mom. And I wanted one of Leo's bear hugs.

Don't start blubbering, you big baby. You'll make Daddy feel bad. But I wanted Mom and Leo so much that squeezing my eyes shut didn't stop the tears.

"Hey, what's this?" Daddy handed me his handkerchief. I blew my nose and tried to stop sniffling.

Daddy put his arm around my shoulder. "It's my fault," he said. "I should have warned you, watched you."

"It's okay," I said trying to smile. "You came back."

Neither one of us said anything for a while. Then all of the questions I wanted to ask Daddy started bobbing around in my head. "What's the matter?" he asked me.

I took a deep breath. I knew if I didn't ask him now, I never would. So I asked, "How come you said it was okay for me to change my name to Zanin?"

"Don't you want to?" Daddy sounded surprised.

Now what do I do? When I finally get up enough guts to ask him the big question, he answers me with a question. "I don't know," I yelled, and jumped up off the couch. I couldn't stop crying as I ran into the bathroom.

"Erin, let me in, please."

"You can come in," I said, but I wished I could disappear. How did I get myself in this mess? Now Daddy was mad at me for sure.

I looked up at him. He was frowning. I knew he was going to yell. "Can we talk?" he asked. The way he asked it made me smile, a little.

Daddy sat down next to me on the couch. He cleared his throat. And then he cleared it again as if a giant frog were stuck inside. "It's a long story, what happened between your mom and me." Daddy got up and walked across the room. He kept pulling on his beard. Then he sat down at his desk and looked down at all my pictures.

My stomach was feeling very funny. What if I was getting appendicitis? Daddy wouldn't know what to do. I took a deep breath and wished the funny feeling away.

"Your letters always sounded happy," Daddy said, "so I thought I made the right decision, staying away." He walked over to the window, opened the blinds, and stared out at the ocean for a while. Then he said, "When Leo and your mother wrote and asked if Leo could adopt you, I thought about it for a long time."

For a few minutes, Daddy didn't say anything else. Then he turned around and looked at me. "I said yes, because I thought you might feel more comfortable with the same name as your mom and Leo. And, I was sure you'd want to change your name when you told me about the twins. But," Daddy pulled at his beard again, "I should have known you'd feel hurt. I'm sorry."

"It's okay." He looked so sad, I gave him a hug.

"Have you decided what you want to do about your name?" he asked.

I could tell Daddy was nervous because his voice was high and squeaky. I started chewing on my thumbnail. I didn't know what to say. My face must have looked funny because Daddy hugged me and said, "Never mind, pretend I didn't ask that question."

But he did ask it. And I didn't know what the answer should be.

"You look a little tired," Daddy said. "Why don't you take a nap. I could use one myself."

"I didn't get the shells for Mom, Leo, and Catherine."

"Storms don't last too long around here. We'll have time later."

Daddy was right. The sun came out in an hour and we went back to the beach. Baby waves rolled up to the shore and the sky was a light blue. We hunted for seashells. I found a sand dollar for Leo, a pearly green star shell for Catherine, and a baby-bonnet shell for Mom.

Walking along the beach, Daddy and I started talking. He told me he was leaving Florida next week for Australia. "And then," he said in a quiet voice, "I'm going to England to photograph castles for another book."

"How long will you be gone?"

"About a year." Daddy put his arm around my shoulder. "Will you visit me when I get back?"

A year. In a year, I'll be almost thirteen. The twins might be walking. Maybe even talking. I'll look different. And Daddy won't know how I've changed because he'll have this year's pictures. He'll never know the everyday me the way Mom and Leo do.

And we'll never talk. I won't be able to call him if he's off in an old castle somewhere or chasing koala bears in Australia.

"I'll visit you." I began digging a hole in the sand with my toe.

"And you'll keep on writing to me, won't you?" Daddy held onto my hand and looked at me as if he were trying to memorize every part of my face.

"I'll write," I answered. A warm breeze blew my hair around my face, but I felt shivery as we started back.

That night I couldn't sleep, thoughts kept buzzing around my head like a pack of hungry mosquitoes. I opened the blinds and watched the lights blinking out on the ocean. Maybe they could tell me what to do. One blink for Zanin. Two blinks for Mitchell.

Boy. Talk about stupid. I got up and took my lucky penny out of my purse. I blew on it and tossed it. Heads for Zanin. Tails for Mitchell.

Heads. I guess I'll be Erin Zanin. I crawled back into bed and thought about it. Maybe I'll get used to it. I rolled the name *Erin Zanin* round and round in my head. Mom and Leo will be happy. Leo is really my everyday dad, anyway. Daddy is more like a friend. He's too far away to even be a sometimes dad.

Zanin. Erin Zanin. I sat up and hugged my knees. Erin Zanin just didn't sound right. It didn't sound like me. The funny part was it didn't have anything to do with Leo.

But it had everything to do with me.

Seventeen

It was almost time to leave for the airport. I checked out all my stuff while Daddy was in the kitchen drinking a last-minute cup of coffee. Everything was in my purse, including Ryan's gum, my lucky penny, and the silver-blue eye shadow. I decided not to wear it. No sense making Mom mad my first day home.

When Daddy came out of the kitchen, he was carrying a package. "I don't wrap too well." He handed me a flat box wrapped in gold paper, grinned at me, and said, "But I try."

"It's pretty. What is it?"

"You'll see. But you can't open it until the plane takes off. Promise."

"I promise. But couldn't you give me a little hint?"

"No hints." Daddy laughed and shook his head.

What could be in the box? It was heavy, but not too heavy, and it didn't rattle. What if the airport security made me open it? I'd die if they thought I was a mad bomber.

It didn't take too long to get to the airport. No bells rang when we passed through the security check, but I thought the lady gave me a funny look.

I still didn't know what to tell Daddy about my name change and I didn't know how to say good-bye. I felt stupid and a little scared.

Daddy didn't say anything, either. He just kept his arm around my shoulders. When they announced, "Flight Number 73 now boarding for O'Hare International Airport," Daddy leaned over and kissed my cheek. "See you next year?"

I nodded. Daddy squeezed my shoulders hard. "I'm glad we had this time together, Erin. Tell your mother she did a super job on you. You're a very special girl." Daddy smiled at me. "You won't forget to write, will you?"

"No." I reached up, put my arms around Daddy's neck

and kissed his cheek. "Good-bye, Daddy," I said. "Thank you for a good time and the presents."

I kept turning around and waving until I reached the door of the airplane. It's so weird when you feel sad and glad at the same time. Saying good-bye to Daddy was hard, but I was ready to go home. I missed everybody. Well, almost everybody. I didn't miss Kim Adams and her crowd.

I didn't feel as twitchy as last time, but I made sure the barf bag was near my seat, just in case. No one was sitting next to me, so I put Daddy's package on the seat and checked out my purse. I had this feeling I might have left my lucky penny on Daddy's desk, but it was at the bottom of my purse. I gave it a quick rub for good luck. Ryan's gum was there, too. I popped a piece in my mouth and looked around. Boring. No kids. No cute guys, just people in business suits.

When the plane started to move, I opened Daddy's package. There was a note on top of a book. It said:

Dear Erin,

Please turn to the inside page and read the dedication. I hope you like it. I also have enclosed copies of the pictures I took of you. Pick out the one you want me to have enlarged. I plan to put it next to your picture that's on the wall in my den.

Write to me soon. My address is always the same no matter where I am. I'll be calling you. Don't forget I'm counting on next year.

Love,

Daddy

P.S. Try not to worry about the name change. You'll find your own answer.

Where? I wondered.

I looked at the book. The cover was a photo of kites flying in a blue sky. I traced the title, *Places I've Been*, by Paul Mitchell, with my finger.

The dedication said, *To Erin, whose place is always in my heart. With love, Daddy.*

My eyes got so blurry I couldn't see. I guess you can love from far away.

When the plane landed, I walked down the ramp, hoping Mom and Leo would be there. They were. They both gave me a bear hug.

"Did you have a good time?" Mom asked.

"It was fun."

"I missed you," Mom said.

"Me, too." Leo gave me another hug. They both kissed me again. It was really mushy.

While we were waiting for my suitcase to come around

on the conveyor belt, my stomach gave out a loud rumble.
"I couldn't eat the airplane stew," I said. "It had peas in
it . . . a million peas. It was gross."

"How about a pizza at Dino's?" Leo asked, as he
grabbed my suitcase.

At Dino's we ordered cheese and sausage pizza. I could
eat only two pieces. My stomach filled up right away.

Mom and Leo said they'd have their second cup of
coffee at home. *Thank you, God.* I couldn't have sat there
for another minute. I had to call Jenny and find out what
was going on.

Jenny's line was busy. I tried four times, then I gave
up and unpacked my suitcase.

Mom and Leo liked their seashells. They put them on
the piano. That's our special collection place. I showed
them Daddy's book, the dedication, and the pictures
Daddy took of me. Mom hugged me and sort of sighed.

Leo said, "I'm glad you had a good time, punkin."

I wanted to tell Mom and Leo more about Florida, but
I felt funny talking about Daddy. I even wanted to tell
them the almost-drowning part, but I couldn't. They'd
be mad at Daddy for sure.

"Where's Catherine?" I asked.

"She's at her garden-club meeting," Mom answered.
"You can see her tomorrow. Better get ready for bed. You
have school tomorrow."

110

"But I have to talk to Jenny."

"Five minutes."

"Five minutes! M-o-m."

"No more than five minutes." Mom set the timer before she left the room.

"You're back!" Jenny yelled.

"Tell me what's going on at school."

"Nothing much. Old Miss Stuck-up Kim has detention. She talked back to the lunchroom ladies. David Peters said Mr. Hansen called her father. And we lost the basketball game because you weren't there."

"Yeah, right," I said. But it made me feel good. "Tell me about Richard and Ryan."

"I haven't seen them. But wait until I tell you about Amy's new boyfriend. He's more than awesome, he's the absolute."

"You always say that about Amy's boyfriends. What's his name?"

"Jeremy. Isn't that a romantic name?"

"Uh-huh. Tell me more about school."

"We're having a spelling bee tomorrow."

I groaned. "Which words?"

"All of them."

"You're joking. Couldn't Mrs. Lewis be arrested for cruel and unusual punishment?"

Jenny laughed. "It sounds good to me."

"I've got to go, Jen. The timer just went off. I'll see you at the corner tomorrow."

The next morning, I got up early and tried to cram a year's worth of spelling words into my head. They didn't fit.

I waited at the corner for Jenny. She was late. "Hey, Mitchell." I turned around. David Peters was riding past the corner. "See you at school," he said.

Where was Richard? They always ride together.

Jenny was out of breath when she came running up to the corner. I took off my white mirrored sunglasses and gave them to her. "I lost yours," I said.

"How did you lose them?"

"I don't know. I just did."

"Erin, come on. How did you lose them?" Jenny persisted.

I told her. Jenny grabbed my arm. "You almost drowned!" she shrieked. "What did your mom and stepdad say?"

"Nothing. I didn't tell them." Talking about almost drowning made me feel squirmy inside, so I changed the subject. "Can you come over after school? I'll show you what I got."

"Okay," Jenny said. "Come on. We're going to be late."

Ryan was waiting for me at my locker. It was the strangest thing, but I felt almost shy when I saw him. He looked taller, cuter than I remembered. I could feel

112

my face getting red. I felt like he could read my mind. Maybe he knew I dreamed that he kissed me.

Chill out, Mitchell, I scolded myself. Don't be a jerk. If you don't tell anybody about your dream, there's no way they can find out.

"Where's my postcard?" Ryan asked.

"I don't know. I mailed it two days ago. Oh, Ryan, thanks for the gum. It really helped."

"Want some more?" Ryan handed me another pack of Double Bubble. He didn't say anything about his picture and neither did I. Maybe I'll keep it in my wallet.

"Did you hear about Looney Lewis's spelling bee?"

"I'm not ready," I groaned.

"Who is?"

When the bell rang, Ryan said, "See ya, Mitchell," and winked at me. My heart did a hop, skip, and a jump.

In the lunch line, David Peters gave me a noogie on the back of my head. "Richard wants you to call him, Mitchell."

"Why?" How come Richard can't talk for himself, I thought. And why doesn't he call me? Then I felt guilty for thinking that way about Richard Fraizer.

"Richard has the chicken pox," David said. "Call him tonight."

"I don't know if I can." I can't tell him Mom has this thing about calling guys just to talk. I know Mom's living in the last century, but I hate to get her mad.

"You better call him, Mitchell. See ya around."

Now what do I do? I don't even know what I want to do. I headed for my doom in Mrs. Lewis's class.

"Look who's back: Stick," Kim Adams said. She poked Andrea and asked, "Did you ever see a sunburnt stick?" Andrea giggled.

Mrs. Lewis looked up and frowned. Kim and Andrea shut up. I ignored them. We lined up for the spelling bee. I stood next to Matt Anderson and Laurie Contro. Ryan was on my side, too. Kim, Andrea, Jenny, and David Peters were on the other team.

Kim missed the first word, "language." She tried to act like Miss Cool when she sat down, but I know how stupid you feel when you go down on the first word.

I couldn't believe I stayed up for five turns. I even spelled "attentively" right. I think Mrs. Lewis was ready to faint. She gave me one of her twitchy little smiles. "Mechanic" sent me down, but Matt knew how to spell it, so our team won.

"Good job, Mitchell." Ryan shook my hand. It made me feel good.

"Good job, Mitchell," bounced around my head for the rest of the afternoon. During science, I kept sneaking looks at Ryan's picture. While Mrs. Lewis wrote the science assignment on the board, I wrote Ryan's name on my folder. Then I wrote *Erin Mitchell and Ryan Wil-*

liams. I drew a heart around our names. I wondered if Ryan ever wrote my name.

David Peters was waiting for me at my locker after school. "Don't forget to call Richard." He gave my arm a good poke.

"No," I said.

"What's your problem, Mitchell?"

"No problem. Richard can call *me* if he wants to talk." I walked away. Anyway, I thought, running out the door, I'd rather talk to Ryan.

Eighteen

When I came home from school, I found a note from Mom on the refrigerator. It said,

> Hi, Erin,
>   I'll be back from the doctor's around 5:00. I've declared your room a disaster area. Please straighten it, especially the closet. I couldn't tell the clean clothes from the dirty ones.
>   Thank you,
>   Love ya,
>   Mom

I shoved the magazines and shoes under my bed. In the closet, I started piling my dirty clothes into a laundry basket. I found a couple of notes from Jenny on the floor so I scrounged around looking for more notes. I didn't think Mom would read my notes, but just in case she'd be tempted, I thought I better make sure I found all of them.

While I was looking for more notes, I pushed back my clothes and saw my name on the back wall of the closet.

I stared at my name. Then I traced it with my finger. How could I change my name? I couldn't change it any more than I could change the color of my eyes. Just like that, I knew my name was a part of me.

What I didn't know was how I was going to tell Mom and Leo. Maybe if I don't say anything, they won't say anything. And then I can just go on being Erin Mitchell.

I had a funny feeling that wouldn't work. What was I going to do? I closed my eyes and wished I could stay in the closet forever. But that wouldn't work, either. Mom and Leo would find me and want to know why I was sitting on the floor of my closet staring at the wall. They might even think I was sick in the head or something and take me to a doctor.

"I can't win." I pounded my fists on the floor. Lincoln poked his head into the closet. I guess he wondered what was going on. He came over and licked my cheek and I buried my nose in his fur.

117

"What should I do, Lincoln?" He barked. The doorbell was ringing. I knew it was Jenny. So much for hiding out in the closet.

"Did you call?" Jenny asked when I opened the door. "I couldn't wait for you after school. I had to go to the store for my mom. I've been dying to know if you called Richard."

"I'm not going to call him."

"You're kidding," Jenny said.

"I told David that Richard could call me."

"Wow. What turned you into Miss Independence?"

"I don't know." I shrugged. "My mom has a fit if I call boys just to talk and besides, I'm sick of David always talking for Richard. Richard has a mouth of his own."

Jenny didn't act surprised when I told her I like Ryan, a little. I wanted to tell her about my name, but I didn't. Jenny isn't a blabber, but she might let it slip out. Mom and Leo would flip if they heard I wanted to stay Erin Mitchell from Jenny.

I started feeling twitchy again while I was showing Jenny the Florida Beach Bunny shirts. I told her I had cramps. I didn't think God would count that as a lie because I did have a cramp in my head from trying to figure out how to tell Mom and Leo.

Jenny gets cramps, too, so she said she'd go home. "I'll talk to you tomorrow," she said. "Thanks for the presents." I gave her the silver-blue eye shadow, too. It looks better on her than me. I'm going to try tawny beige next.

After Jenny left, I ran over to Catherine's. Catherine liked her pearl green seashell. She said it looked just perfect next to her jade plant.

As usual, Catherine made us some tea. She'd found a new one, apple and cinnamon. I made raisin toast. I managed to swallow two bites of toast before I told her about Florida and me.

"I know who I am," I said. "I found out for sure in my closet. I'm Erin Mitchell, I can't change my name. It's me."

Catherine smiled at me and put down her teacup. "I thought you might feel that way," she said.

Right then, right there in Catherine's kitchen a monster panic wave hit me. How did I think I could tell Mom and Leo? I was a genuine nerd, a dork, and a real jerk. I started biting my lip.

"What's the matter, Erin?" Catherine asked.

"I'm scared to tell Mom and Leo."

"Why?" Catherine shook her head. "They'll understand."

"What if they don't?" I didn't want to think about Mom and Leo looking at me with sad eyes. What if Mom started crying, it would be my fault. I squeezed a raisin out of my toast. "It would be easier," I looked down at the raisin and pushed it back into my toast, "to be a Zanin. Mom and Leo would be happy. And," I gave a great big sigh, "Daddy doesn't mind if I change my name."

"But what about you, Erin? You mind," Catherine said slowly. She frowned. "It takes courage to be who you are," she said. "I know you and I know you have the courage to do it. Tell you mother and Leo the truth."

I decided to tell Mom and Leo before dinner; otherwise, I might throw up the hamburgers Leo was going to grill. I opened my mouth to tell them, but nothing came out. I started to shake. I couldn't do it. I couldn't tell them.

Mom looked at me and frowned. "Are you sick, Erin?" Mom felt my forehead.

"No." My voice squeaked.

"What's the matter? You're not yourself."

But I was and that was the whole trouble.

I decided to go for it, otherwise my name would be chicken instead of Mitchell. Okay. This is it. Tell them. I started with Florida and Daddy. Mom gave a funny little gasp when I told her the almost-drowning part. And then I said in one big breath, "I can't get adopted and be a Zanin. I wouldn't be me."

Mom and Leo didn't say anything. It was so quiet I thought I'd explode. They hated me. I started to blubber like a stupid little kid.

Leo came over to me and gave me a bear hug. "It's okay."

120

"No, it isn't. You hate me. I won't take your name."

"Erin," Leo said in a stern voice, "we're a family. And names don't make a family. Love does."

"I feel bad." I sniffled into his shoulder.

Mom rubbed the back of my head. "We love you," she said.

"I just had to be who I am," I answered.

Leo wiped away the tear that was tickling my nose. "And who are you, punkin?" he asked softly.

"Erin Mitchell. Your daughter." I really suprised myself when the words "your daughter" popped out of my mouth. But I knew it was true. Leo was my everyday dad. And Daddy . . . he was my once-a-year faraway dad. And I was me, Erin Mitchell.

I couldn't wait to tell Jenny.

Printed in the United States
6281